Creating Me!

My Power, Perfection & Life

Supreme Health
Staff & Scientist

Kareem Tyree
Khalil Malik

Gabriella Monique

Creating Me!

Supreme Health and Fitness by Sean Ali!

Achieving and Maintaining Supreme Health and Fitness by Increasing the Level of Knowledge and Science of Life!

A LifeStlye MoveMent!

Be perfect, therefore, as your heavenly Father is perfect.

Matthew 5:48

PAGE 4

Supreme Health & Fitness!   Knowledge Of Self Series Vol 5!

Table of Contents

PAGE 5

Supreme Health & Fitness!   Knowledge Of Self Series Vol 5!

5 Daily Reminders

1. I am amazing.
2. I can do anything.
3. Positivity is a choice.
4. I celebrate my individuality.
5. I am prepared to succeed.

Creating Me!

Introduction!

.....

Peace and Blessings of Health!

This small book represents the 5ᵗʰ Exciting Volume of the Knowledge of Self Series and is the accompanying Work-Book that we will use to Create YourSelf ..... Creating Me .... My Power, Perfection and Life!

Unfortunately for many of us, we have spent our lives creating and claiming our imperfections, our failures and our short-comings, literally rendering ourselves powerless in our own lives.

It seems that there is a predominant idea that makes people feel as if they are egotistical, conceited or in some type of opposition with/to God by simply creating, accepting and claiming our Power and Perfection.

In scripture we are given a command, Matthew 548, where we are ordered to be perfect, even as our father in heaven is perfect.

PAGE 7

Supreme Health & Fitness!   Knowledge Of Self Series Vol 5!

Creating Me!

This is based on scripture and is taking as a direct order or command from God. The idea that you are not perfect, or that nobody can be perfect, is diametrically opposed to what God wants from us and created us to be and do.

So, with this book, entitled creating me, we will use different activities to outline a paradigm shift in ourselves and in our thinking about ourselves.

We will lay the foundation where we can see the Value, the Strength, the characteristics of Power and Greatness in ourselves. We want to be able to create ourselves into the exact person that we want to be.

There is only ONE of YOU on this planet earth, which means that there is absolutely NO ONE that you can compare yourself to point out any imperfections. Whatever you have an whoever you are is uniquely manifested in you and by you.

You are already the Perfect You!

You are already Powerful!

With this book we will Use the activities to strengthen and to solidify the natural gifts and qualities that we are already in possession.

When you were a baby, it was you that learned how to strengthen your neck muscles and control them to hold your head up.

PAGE 8

Supreme Health & Fitness!   Knowledge Of Self Series Vol 5!

Creating Me!

It was you that taught yourself how to crawl. And once you accomplish these, you then taught yourself how to pull yourself up.

Through each of these stages you gained power and mastery over yourself. To the point where you developed the strength to not only hold your head up, to not only pull yourself up, but to also move yourself where you wanted to go.

Do you know that everything in your life is this **sum total** of what you wanted to do??

That's right, except for respiration, digestion, hearing and smell, every other movement in your body is caused by YOU!

This is neither good nor bad, it's indicative of how powerful you are and how you create an effect on your life. It's why you are where you are at right now because of you.

See, many of you will look at your life right now and you will think that because it's not what you wanted to be right now that you are a failure or imperfect.

But no, you just have to learn how to express your power to achieve the results that you want.

PAGE 9

Supreme Health & Fitness!   Knowledge Of Self Series Vol 5!

Creating Me!

How you feel about yourself, how you think about yourself how you introduce and tell people about yourself is the foundation for the moves and actions that you make.

If you know that you are powerful ... if you know that you are perfect ... if you know that it's up to you when it comes to your life, all of these will help you to make choices and moves that are conducive to your growth and development .

The main thing is that you will be Empowered. That you will be Decisive. That you will NOT sit in wait, wasting your time and your life, waiting for somebody to come and do for you that which only you can do for yourself.

Now if you do not know how powerful you are, if you do not know that you are perfect, if you do not know that your life is up to you - then you are in a state powerlessness. This state self-imposed, so you have rendered yourself powerless.

So. if you need healing or you need to improve the quality of your life or you want to create your heaven and set yourself in it at once - the catalyst for success or failure lies in how you view yourself.

The only thing a Health care professional can do is to help you create the proper Healthy environment IN you that allows your Body to HEAL ITSELF ...

PAGE 10

Supreme Health & Fitness!   Knowledge Of Self Series Vol 5!

Creating Me!

Although our Physical Body is created with the necessary Elements to heal itself, the basis of Healing begins WITHIN THE MIND!!

The Purpose of this book is to lay the Foundation of Mental and Spiritual Healing by Building the Will and Strengthening and Increasing Mental Power with Written and Physical Activities.

There can be NO WRONG Answers and you are Guaranteed Absolute SUCCESS.!!!!!

In fact, YOU WILL GET BACK EACTLY 100% OF WHAT YOU PUT IN!!!!

You will be writing Your own Great Story of Excellence, Power, Health and Love that will help u to successfully carry You into the Enjoyment of Abundant Life!!!!

Some of what we want to accomplish with this volume includes creating a new Definition of ourselves – based on HOW we see ourselves instead of others. We also want to accomplish Intentional Learning about ourselves. Unfortunately, many of us don not know ourselves and can only define ourselves according to how others define us.

We have a dual track processing mind where our brain processes and creates memories in 2 distinct ways, Implicit and Explicit.

PAGE 11

Supreme Health & Fitness!   Knowledge Of Self Series Vol 5!

Creating Me!

Everything that you will see, hear or encounter is stored as a memory.

So, as we move throughout life, if we encounter similar situations our brain will take search for one of these previous memories to try to figure out a solution or determine what to do. This is our implicit form of using memories.

We cannot control this because everything that our senses intake is naturally and immediately stored.

This includes how we view ourselves. The first memories we have of ourselves comes from other people, usually our parents or guardians. They talk to us and tell us how they feel about us and describe to us how they view us and what they want us to be, all of which is stored in created in our implicit memory storage.

Unfortunately, many parents do not instill into their children that they are perfect.

Also, many parents are not equipped to teach their children the information contained in this book that will foster in them a sense of their own power in greatness. which in turn would allow them to grow into their power so that they can manifest it and be great.

So, these children are growing and developing without a sense of their power, become adults that lack this same knowledge of power.

PAGE 12

Supreme Health & Fitness!   Knowledge Of Self Series Vol 5!

Creating Me!

This creates the cycle of underachievement and self-destruction that we see prevalent throughout the world.

When you came out of the womb of your mother and the doctor or health care professional that held you as you came out, examined you and declared you healthy and perfect, then handed you to your parents.

So, how did you lose your natural perfection. Think about this, if the 1st 3 or 4 people that saw you when you came into the world declared you perfect, how can you as an adult with the ability to speak in describe yourself now see yourself as imperfect.

How did you lose your perfection .... or did you?

Did you lose your perfection or is it that you never declared it ??

Did you lose your perfection or is it the case of you not claiming you're perfection ???

Did you lose your perfection, or have you simply not created it???

Included in this Volume are several activities and exercises that you can use to create or build on your Self-Awareness, that will help you build and increase your Self-Perception and that will help you understand and over-come any FEARS or mis-conceptions that you may have developed about yourself.

Supreme Health & Fitness!   Knowledge Of Self Series Vol 5!

PAGE 13

Creating Me!

With this book, this is our opportunity to create explicit memories of our self. The kind of memories that we want and need to Empower Self!

Remember the implicit memories are those that are a part of our sensory intake, which we have no control over. Those implicit memories that you have of yourself is what has gotten you to where you are right now, you can replace those with the explicit memories that you will create from the activities of this book to take yourself where you want to go.

So, where your implicit memories created the atmosphere that you caused you to think that you are not perfect and cannot be perfect, and caused you to render yourself powerless and accept your failure and your faults ... you will replace these with explicit memories of how Great you are, of how Powerful you are, how Intelligent you are and of how Perfect You Are!

Creating Me .... My Power, Perfection & Life!

You will become able to use your own thinking to create your own Image and Understanding of WHO YOU ARE!

You can use your own Power and Thinking to create your own Healing and Health!

We can use your own Power and Thinking to Successfully Enjoy Abundant Life!

PAGE 14

Supreme Health & Fitness!   Knowledge Of Self Series Vol 5!

Creating Me!

Words have Electrical and Chemical Actions that correspond to their Meaning and Use.

During these activities you have to Think of and apply to yourself the Highest Quality and Power of words. As you Think of them, the Electrical Energy/Current of these words begin to be created IN YOU!

The corresponding Chemical Hormones of the words are being transported throughout your body. You are beginning the process of creating Healing, Health, Life, Power and Perfection IN YOURSELF!

After producing these thoughts, you are now ready to transform your Un- Seen Thoughts INTO a Seen Reality!

Writing is Action ..... Physical Action.

In order for your muscles to Move, an Action Potential or electrical impulse is created which causes your muscles to contract = Motion.

We have Motion the we can Cause - Voluntary and we have Reflex Motion or Involuntary motion, that our body causes on its own. By Writing, you are creating a Determined and Focused Electrical Current to Move yourself.

PAGE 15

Supreme Health & Fitness!   Knowledge Of Self Series Vol 5!

Creating Me!

Your body begins to coordinate Motion, which is the physical expression of your un-seen Thought. The same way the thought of eating causes you to Move – manifesting into the Act of eating to make that thought reality.

In this case, you are using your Thought to produce the Actins that Causes your Healing, Health, Life, Power and Perfection by first Thinking. That thought will then Cause the Motion of yourself.

The Effect of your motion is manifested in your being Healed, the Improvement of the Quality of your Life, your Empowerment and you are your Perfected Self!!!!

The Act of Writing about Your own Healing, Health, Life and Power creates the environment where you BECOME that which you are Writing!

As a Man Thinketh – So IS he!

Lastly, you actively Talk to yourself. You will LOOK at your reflection and communicate with yourself and reinforce your Power.

While doing this, you are activating and engaging your Sense of Sight/Vision ... Seeing Yourself SAY these empowering statements of stimuli.

PAGE 16

Supreme Health & Fitness!   Knowledge Of Self Series Vol 5!

Creating Me!

You are engaging your Hearing .... Hearing statements of Healing, Health, Life and Power BEAT into your eardrum and immediately impacting your Brain, Mind and Thoughts.

Your Ears are connected directly to your Brain! So, when you read your words in this book, the Energy goes directly to your Control Center – Your Brain!

You are Creating your Healing, Health, Life and Power by speaking into existence your own Story – Produced from your own Thoughts.

This is your Book of Life!

We all need inspiration from time to time. So, instead of using another person's story for Inspiration or Motivation – you can Open Your Own Book and draw Inspiration, Motivation and Power from YOURSELF!!!!!

CREATING is the ACTION stage of Life......

The Best way to Create is to Write .... Then you simply LIVE that which you WRITTEN!

Now you have your tool to Create – in the form of this book!

You have the science to Create – in the form of the activities!

PAGE 17

Supreme Health & Fitness!   Knowledge Of Self Series Vol 5!

Creating Me!

Now all you have to do is get In ACTION!!!!

Open Your Book and Start CREATING!!!

Create Your Power!!!

Create Your Perfection!!!

Create Your Life and GO BE GREAT!!!

Creating Me ..... My Power, Perfection & Life!!!

Peace!

Sean Ali

PAGE 18

Supreme Health & Fitness!   Knowledge Of Self Series Vol 5!

Creating Me!

hi! today will be . . .

awesome

daily goal

desired outcome

PAGE 20

Supreme Health & Fitness!   Knowledge Of Self Series Vol 5!

SUPPORT SYSTEM

Who can I call when...

I'm feeling lonely:

_____

I need some company:

_____

I need someone to talk to:

_____

I need someone to encourage me to get out of the house and do something fun:

_____

I need someone to remind me to follow my self care plan:

_____

Other:

_____

PAGE 21

Supreme Health & Fitness!　　　　　　　　Knowledge Of Self Series Vol 5!

Name _____   Date _____

POSITIVE THOUGHTS & AFFIRMATIONS

1. There is no one better to be than myself
2. I am enough.
3. I get better every single day
4. I am an amazing person
5. All of my problems have solutions
6. Today I am a leader
7. I forgive myself for my mistakes
8. My challenges help me grow
9. I am perfect just the way I am
10. My mistakes help me learn and grow
11. Today is going to be a great day
12. I have courage and confidence
13. I can control my own happiness
14. I have people who love and respect me.
15. I stand up for what I believe in
16. I believe in my goals and dreams
17. It's okay not to know everything
18. Today I choose to think positive.
19. I can get through anything.
20. I can do anything I put my mind to.
21. I give myself permission to make choices.
22. I can do better next time
23. I have everything I need right now
24. I am capable of so much
25. Everything will be okay.

29. I am free to make my own choices
30. I deserve to be loved.
31. I can make a difference.
32. Today I choose to be confident.
33. I am in charge of my life
34. I have the power to make my dreams true
35. I believe in myself and my abilities.
36. Good things are going to come to me
37. I matter
38. My confidence grows when I step outside of my comfort zone.
39. My positive thoughts create positive feelings
40. Today I will walk through my fears.
41. I am open and ready to learn.
42. Every day is a fresh start
43. If I fall, I will get back up again.
44. I am whole.
45. I only compare myself to myself
46. I can do anything.
47. It is enough to do my best
48. I can be anything I want to be
49. I accept who I am
50. Today is going to be an awesome day

PAGE 22

Supreme Health & Fitness!   Knowledge Of Self Series Vol 5!

PAGE 23

Supreme Health & Fitness!   Knowledge Of Self Series Vol 5!

Chapter One

Developing a Self-Concept

* * * * *

Who are you? What Is the Self?

How has your view of yourself changed over the years?

When we think about Ourselves, we have to 1st go to the root or foundation of HOW our first understanding of Ourselves is created. Our initial beginnings of the ideas of Ourselves are created from external influences.

Newborn babies have no ego boundaries, which define where an individual stops and the rest of the world begins (Chodorow, 1989).

Within the first year or two of life, as infants start to differentiate themselves from the rest of the world, the Self begins to develop.

From babies, to toddlers, then as children, we devote enormous energy to understanding who we are. We will actively seek to define themselves and to become competent in the identities we claim for ourselves.

This is the beginning of a self-concept: the realization that I am a separate entity.

PAGE 24

Supreme Health & Fitness!   Knowledge Of Self Series Vol 5!

Energetic Self Perception

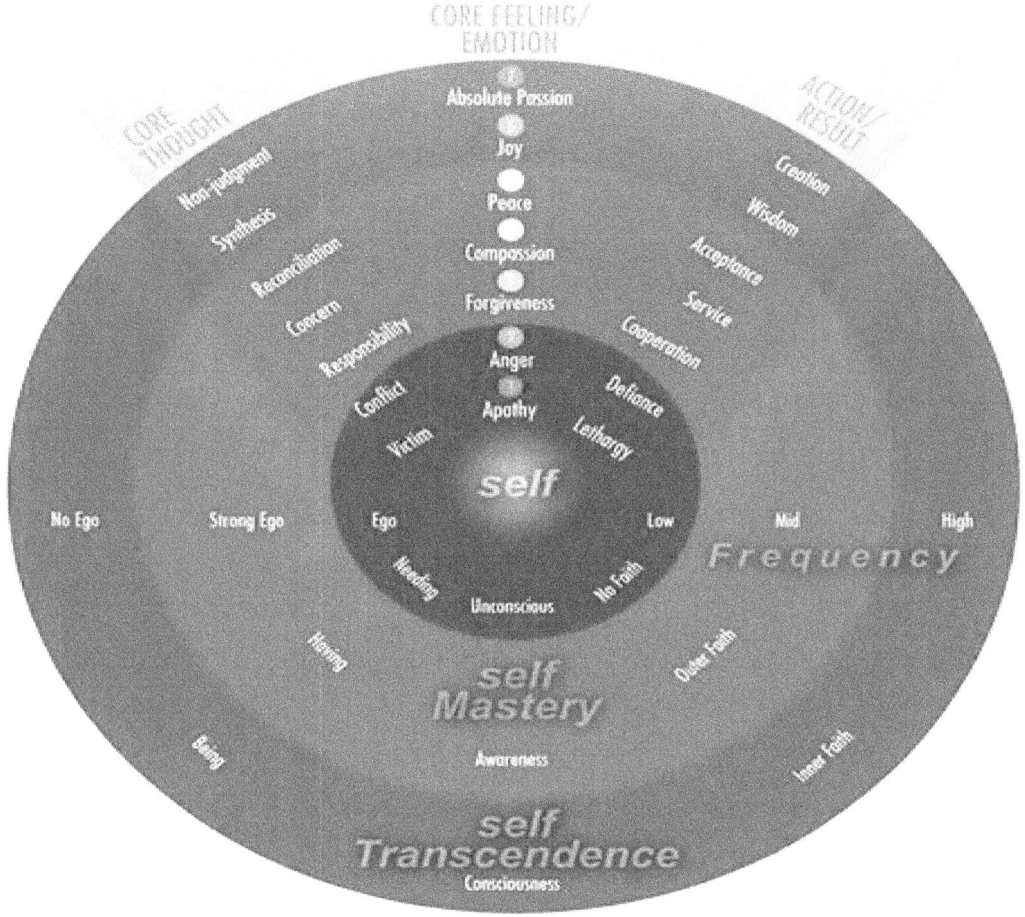

The Self arises in and from communication and it can be considered a multi-dimensional process of internalizing and acting from social perspectives.

According to modern psychology, we develop ourselves by internalizing two kinds of perspectives that are communicated to us: the perspectives of Particular others and the perspective of the Generalized others (Mead, 1934).

Although the word Self can be construed as though it is referring to a single entity, in reality the Self is made up of many dimensions.

The multiple dimensions of Self are shaped and influenced by direct definitions, reflected appraisals, identity scripts, attachment styles, social comparisons, and the perspectives of the generalized other.

Once we know how the image of Ourselves is formulated, we can then examine how we, as individuals, have been shaped and now we have the opportunity to RE-SHAPE Ourselves according to HOW we want to BE!!!!!

- Self Concept
  - Summarizes the beliefs a person holds about his own attributes and how he evaluates the self on these qualities
- Ideal Self
  - A person's conception of how he would like to be
- Actual Self
  - Refers to our more realistic appraisal of the qualities we do and don't have
- Impression Management
  - Our efforts to "manage" what others think of us, choosing products that show us off in a good light

Particular Others

The first perspectives that affects us are those of **Particular Others**. Particular others are specific people who are important in our lives.

PAGE 26

Supreme Health & Fitness!   Knowledge Of Self Series Vol 5!

Creating Me!

For infants and children, the particular others include family members and caregivers. Later in life, particular others will most likely also include peers, teachers, friends, romantic partners, coworkers, and other individuals who are especially important in our lives. As babies interact with particular others in their world, they learn how others see them.

This is the beginning of a self-concept. Notice that the Self starts from outside—from how particular others view us.

Parents and other individuals who matter to us communicate who we are and what we are worth through the concepts of direct definitions, reflected appraisals, scripts, and attachment styles.

Viewpoints of specific people who are significant to us

- mothers
- fathers
- siblings
- aunts / uncles

Direct Definition

As the name implies, direct definition is communication that tells us explicitly who we are by directly labeling us and our behaviors. Family members, as well as peers, teachers, and other individuals, define us by telling us who we are or are expected to be.

Positive direct definitions enhance our self-esteem: "You're smart," "You're strong," "You're great at soccer."

Negative direct definitions can damage children's self-esteem (Brooks & Goldstein, 2001): "You're a troublemaker," "You're stupid," "You're impossible."

Negative messages can and almost always do demolish a child's sense of self-worth.

Positive messages can and almost always do increases a child's sense of self-worth.

Communication that explicitly labels us and our behaviors

- For example, a parent might say
  - "You're my little girl."
  - "You're so responsible."
  - "You're a troublemaker."
  - "You're impossible."

Important individuals in our lives often provide us with direct definitions of our racial and ethnic identities.

In cultures with a majority race, members of minority races often make special efforts to teach children to take pride in the strength and traditions of their racial and ethnic group. Thus, the ethnic training found in many African American families stresses both positive identification with black heritage and awareness of prejudice on the part of people who are not black.

Cultures vary in how they view the self and even in when they believe social identity begins. In the United States, a person is thought to exist at least when biological birth occurs, and many Americans believe that a fetus is a human self. Yet, in some societies, the self does not start at birth—and certainly not prior to birth (Morgan, 1996).

Direct definitions can boost or impair children's self-esteem, growth, development and what type of adult they become and ultimately how they behave and achieve.

Direct definitions lead directly to Reflected Appraisals. From direct definition, children learn what others value in them, and this shapes what they come to value in themselves. They use how others described them to form HOW they describe or view themselves to themselves.

- Reflected Appraisal – perceptions of the judgements of those around us
- Judgements of significant others are especially salient.

- Social Comparison – evaluating ourselves in terms of how we compare to others
- We use reference groups as a basis of comparison.

PAGE 28

Supreme Health & Fitness!   Knowledge Of Self Series Vol 5!

Reflected Appraisal

Reflected appraisal is our perception of another's view of us. How we think others appraise us affects how we see ourselves. This concept is similar to the **looking-glass** self, based on Charles Cooley's poetic comment, "Each to each a looking glass/Reflects the other that doth pass" (1961).

Others are mirrors for us—the views of ourselves that we see in them (our mirrors) shape how we perceive ourselves.

One way to think about reflected appraisals and direct definitions is to realize that others' expressed views of us can elevate or lower our self-concept. People elevate our self-concept when they admire our strengths and accomplishments and accept our weaknesses and problems without discounting us. When we're around these people, we feel more upbeat and positive about ourselves.

REFLECTED APPRAISAL

Others are a mirror for how we see/interpret/evaluate ourselves

Mental Process
- "I think you believe …"
- "I believe you believe …"
- "I know you believe …"

Three Types: Uppers, Downers, Vultures
- Uppers
  - Admire and accept
- Downers
  - Point out and put down
- Vultures
  - Exploit and attach

This is what we want to accomplish with Creating and Building our own Self Definition and Self Appraisal, based on our own Love and Respect of Yourself!

We want to use our own direct definitions of ourselves to establish our own Appraisals of ourselves that will create in us the environment of Healing, Health, Power and Life.

We empower ourselves to be able to turn inward to get the Energy and Power we need to accomplish ALL our goals instea0d of having to depend on others and becoming stuck or rendering ourselves power-LESS.

LIFE PURPOSE WORKSHEET

Why are you alive?	
What are you most proud of having accomplished at this point in your life?	
If you were financially able to retire one year from today, what would you begin working on to prepare for that?	
What would you most like the people at your funeral to say about you, specifically?	
Who in history do you admire most, and why?	
If you could solve a world problem, what would it be? Be VERY specific please.	
What is the inkling you have of your purpose or vision?	
What is in the way of putting this ahead of what you are engaged in now?	
If it weren't important to have a life purpose, what would you most like to do in the next decade?	
List 3 possible life purposes.	1. 2. 3.

Supreme Health & Fitness! Knowledge Of Self Series Vol 5!

PAGE 30

The best way
to predict your
future
is to create it.

YOUR VOICE COMMANDS YOUR MIND, BODY & SPIRIT

Learn the true meaning of each word, the root and the original intention. Find the cousins to each word, say it, feel it, which one will move you forward in your own life?

ENERGY + VIBRATION = MATTER

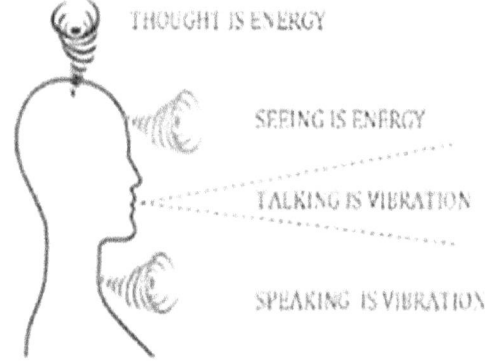

THOUGHT IS ENERGY

SEEING IS ENERGY

TALKING IS VIBRATION

SPEAKING IS VIBRATION

THOUGHTS + VOICE = REALITY

Help the self by Walking the Absolute Truth of your own life, Meditate & Pray...Keep thoughts, actions & words positive...Be self empowered and use the tools presented in a good way

Made with unconditional love
Barbara M. Moreau, Angel who dances on the Clouds
Frank J. Austin, Manybones (Teacher)

I can't I won't It's hard I Don't Believe I'm a skeptic I don't like it	=	• Will literally stop growth • Will literally put a block in your way • Can not is a command to self • Will literally stop you from achieving anything in your life • Is a taught behavior that is a conditional to hold a person back • Stops a person from learning • Stops a person from gaining intellect (IQ)
Try Trying I can try I'm trying I will try I will attempt	=	• Try and you will do it over and over and over never get to the end • Puts a block in your way • Try is a command to self • Try and trying is a taught behavior that is a condition to hold a person back • It has very little or no results • It is like running a race with no end • It is never ending • It is repetitious
I can I am I believe It is done I can do it I can do anything	=	• Literally promotes growth • Can is a command to self • Allows your wants, needs and desire to come true • Is a behavior of using good words • It is unconditional and moves a person forward in life • When you know inside you can do it your body needs to hear it • Your body reacts to key words

PAGE 32

Supreme Health & Fitness!   Knowledge Of Self Series Vol 5!

Self-Development

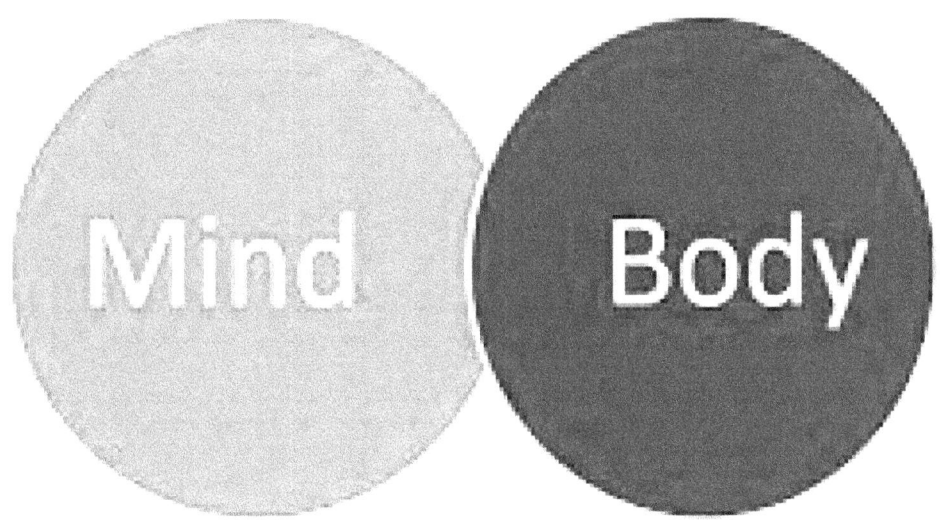

All About Me!

Complete these sentences about yourself. Share with others!

My favorite color is...	My favorite subject is...	I'm most happy when I...
The last movie I watched was...	My favorite food is	I really hate it when...
Yesterday, I...	Most people don't know that I...	If I had a million dollars...
Tomorrow, I will...	Right now, I feel very...	My favorite memory is...

PAGE 34

Supreme Health & Fitness!   Knowledge Of Self Series Vol 5!

Self Care Checklist

- ☐ Overspend, overeat, and overindulge
- ☐ Expect others to read your mind and meet your needs
- ☐ Withhold success from yourself
- ☐ Ignore your deepest desires but seek to fulfill the desires of others
- ☐ Ignore your real emotions and put on a "happy" face
- ☐ Push yourself beyond reasonable limits
- ☐ Allow others to emotionally, physically, or sexually abuse you
- ☐ Deflect compliments
- ☐ Say yes because you can't say no
- ☐ Avoid time alone
- ☐ Over-exhaust yourself because of your need to feel important, needed, or worthy
- ☐ Fear emotional intimacy
- ☐ Try to do it all yourself, never asking for help
- ☐ Try to appear perfect

- ☐ Take time for yourself
- ☐ Allow yourself to make mistakes and to be open about your weaknesses
- ☐ Ask from your needs to be met from a place of vulnerability
- ☐ Spend time with friends
- ☐ Rest
- ☐ Play
- ☐ Exercise
- ☐ Eat well
- ☐ Spend money wisely
- ☐ Pursue your dreams
- ☐ Share honestly with others
- ☐ Enjoy and make time to enjoy and be intimate with those you love
- ☐ Forgive
- ☐ Allow others to be disappointed in you
- ☐ Appropriately express emotions, including anger and sadness
- ☐ Tell others what they mean to you
- ☐ Be present for your children
- ☐ Receive love from others
- ☐ Say yes and no
- ☐ Create a powerful support system for yourself
- ☐ Celebrate accomplishments big and small

OR
do you ↗

PAGE 35

Supreme Health & Fitness!   Knowledge Of Self Series Vol 5!

Creating Me!

_____'s Self-Assessment

Why Complete a Self-Assessment?

Completing a self-assessment takes a snapshot of your life, where you are at right now, and helps you to determine what's important to you at this moment.

Directions

In each space, reflect on what's going on in your life in each of these parts of your life. Write a few words or phrases that capture what it is happening or needs to change.

Measuring Progress

In a few months (and without looking at previous self-assessments) complete another one to see where you are at. What changed? How are things the same or different? What do you want to work on?

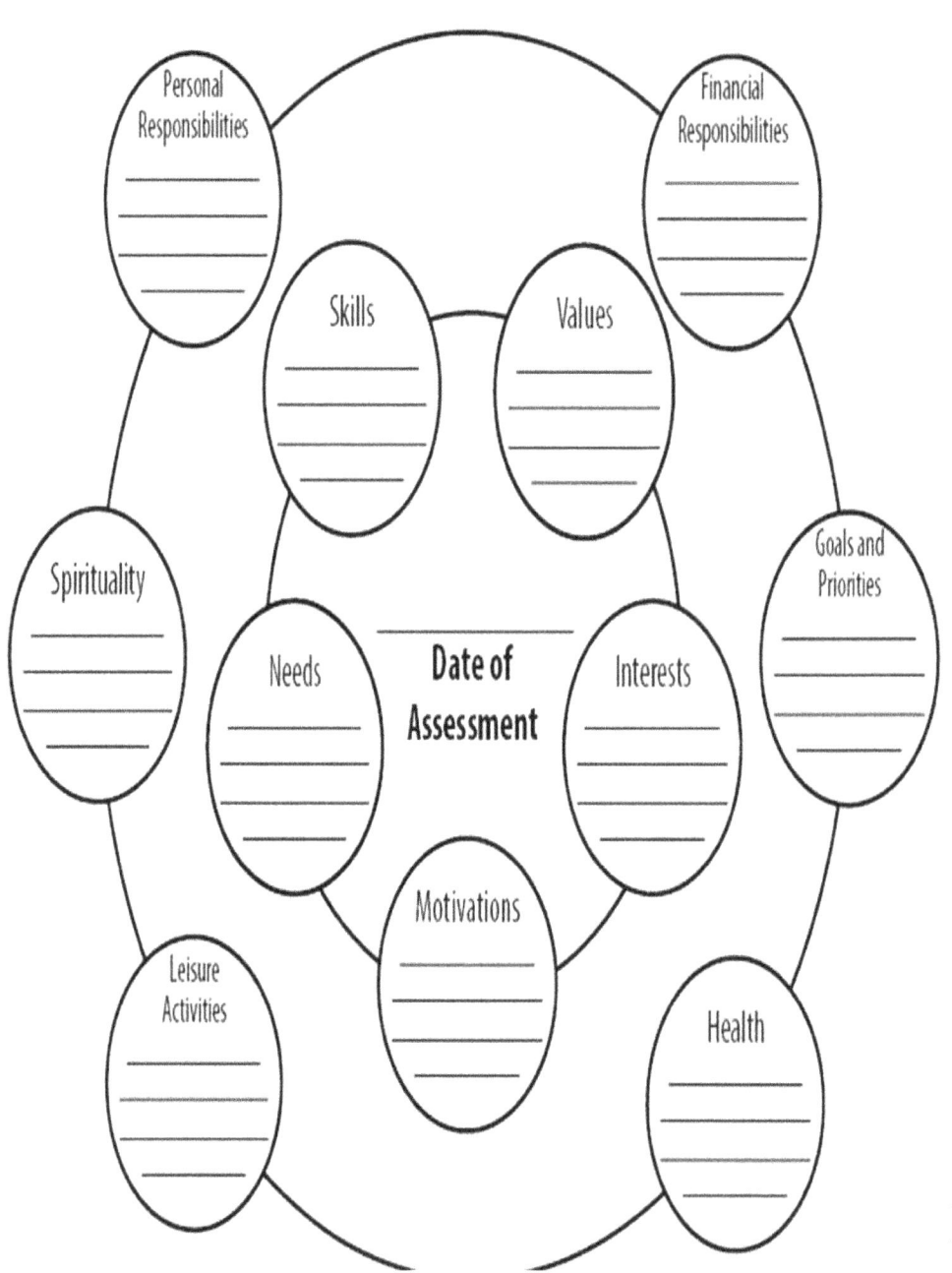

Creating Me!

Draw a self portrait

WHO AM I?

Full Name

Places I have lived

Course and Section:
Graduating Class
Major
Minor(s)
Birthday
Hobbies and extra-curricular activities

Most memorable recent event

An accomplishment I am proud of

Person I look up to

Pets

I have never

Qualities of a good math teacher

Something interesting about myself

Favorite

Color

Artist/Song

Sports Team

Food

TV Show

Class taken

Book

Movie

Self-Awareness Test

To determine your own level of awareness, read the items below and place a check mark (Y) in the blank which you think describes how often you feel this way.

	Always	Frequently	Sometimes	Rarely	Never
I'm eager to learn					
I am excited about working.					
I'm willing to listen with an open mind.					
I constantly have new ideas.					
I like taking direction from people who know something I don't.					
I try to look at the world through the eyes of the other person.					
I believe each person is unique.					

Supreme Health & Fitness!   Knowledge Of Self Series Vol 5!

PAGE 38

My Strengths and Qualities

Things I am good at:

1
_____

2
_____

3
_____

Compliments I have received:

1
_____

2
_____

3
_____

What I like about my appearance:

1
_____

2
_____

3
_____

Challenges I have overcome:

1
_____

2
_____

3
_____

I've helped others by:

1
_____

2
_____

3
_____

Things that make me unique:

1
_____

2
_____

3
_____

What I value the most:

1
_____

2
_____

3
_____

Times I've made others happy:

1
_____

2
_____

3
_____

Life Satisfaction

How satisfied are you with your life?

Give a SCORE, out of 10, for how SATISFIED you are with your life overall. (10 is very satisfied)

1   2   3   4   5   6   7   8   9   10

Give a SCORE for how much FUN you are having in life. (10 means lots of fun!)

1   2   3   4   5   6   7   8   9   10

Is there an area of your life that you could make more exciting? Briefly describe.

4. What areas of your life do you want to improve? I want to:

- ☐   Improve my relationship.
- ☐   Heal my heart.
- ☐   Understand my life purpose.
- ☐   Learn to be more efficient with time management
- ☐   Feel more confident.
- ☐   Change, or move forwards, my career.
- ☐   Achieve my goals.
- ☐   Be happier in life.
- ☐   Live my life with ease and flow, rather than stress and frustration.
- ☐   Feel more at peace.
- ☐   To Learn to trust myself more/Be my Authentic Self.
- ☐   Other _____

5. I am ready to take ACTION and make changes in my environment, habits and life.

Maybe / Yes / No   (please circle)

PAGE 40

Supreme Health & Fitness!   Knowledge Of Self Series Vol 5!

Self-Esteem Check-Up

Directions: Rate from 0 to 10 how much you believe each statement. '0' means you do not believe it at all and '10' means you completely believe it.

Statement	Rating
1. I believe in myself	_____
2. I am just as valuable as other people	_____
3. I would rather be me than someone else	_____
4. I am proud of my accomplishments	_____
5. I feel good when I get compliments	_____
6. I can handle criticism	_____
7. I am good at solving problems	_____
8. I love trying new things	_____
9. I respect myself	_____
10. I like the way I look	_____
11. I love myself even when others reject me	_____
12. I know my positive qualities	_____
13. I focus on my successes and not my failures	_____
14. I'm not afraid to make mistakes	_____
15. I am happy to be me	_____
Total Score	_____

Overall, how would you rate your self esteem on the following scale:

0 _____10

I completely
dislike who I
am

I completely
like who I am

What would need to change in order for you to move up one point on the rating scale? (i.e. For example, if you rated yourself a "6" what would need to happen for you to be at a "7"?)

_____

_____

_____

Goals and Dreams

What are your goals and dreams?

What are you most passionate about?

Where can you see yourself in ten years?

How I Feel

I feel: _____

Happy	Mad	Sad	Glad
Worried	Excited	Bored	Scared
Annoyed	Upset	Sick	Nervous

I feel this way because:

_____

_____

_____

This is what I did about it:

_____

_____

_____

Something else I could have done is:

_____

_____

_____

Ask for help	Take deep breaths	Walk away
Do something else	Tell an adult	Talk to a friend

Self-Awareness

Please identify where you feel you are currently on the following scales. This will help you become more self-aware of your current situation.

Self Esteem

| Low | 1 | 2 | 3 | 4 | 5 | 6 | 7 | 8 | 9 | 10 | High |

Happiness

| Depressed | 1 | 2 | 3 | 4 | 5 | 6 | 7 | 8 | 9 | 10 | Happy |

Assertiveness

| Timid | 1 | 2 | 3 | 4 | 5 | 6 | 7 | 8 | 9 | 10 | Assertive |

Calmness

| Explosive | 1 | 2 | 3 | 4 | 5 | 6 | 7 | 8 | 9 | 10 | Calm |

Life Stresses

| Out of Control | 1 | 2 | 3 | 4 | 5 | 6 | 7 | 8 | 9 | 10 | Controlled |

Time Management

| Disorganised | 1 | 2 | 3 | 4 | 5 | 6 | 7 | 8 | 9 | 10 | Organised |

PAGE 44

Supreme Health & Fitness!   Knowledge Of Self Series Vol 5!

Creating Me!

SELF- ESTEEM WORKSHEET

NAME_____SLS1301C – Life Career Planning

DEFINE SELF -ESTEEM:

List 10 adjectives, positive or negative that YOU think describe you. Ex. I am creative. I am stubborn.

1._____ 6._____

2._____ 7._____

3._____ __ 8._____

4._____ 9._____

5._____ 10._____

List 4 of your strengths:

1._____

2._____

3._____

4._____

List 4 of your weaknesses/challenges:

1._____

2._____

3._____

4._____

PAGE 45

Supreme Health & Fitness!   Knowledge Of Self Series Vol 5!

How Can I Improve?

Name:_____

Date: _____

Currently I can

_____

I need to improve

_____

My goal is to

_____

List ways to reach your goal:

1._____

2._____

3._____

4._____

5._____

I will achieve the goal on this date:

Supreme Health & Fitness!   Knowledge Of Self Series Vol 5!

PAGE 46

5 Daily Reminders

1. I am amazing.
2. I can do anything.
3. Positivity is a choice.
4. I celebrate my individuality.
5. I am prepared to succeed.

PAGE 47

Supreme Health & Fitness!   Knowledge Of Self Series Vol 5!

Chapter Two

Creating Self Improvement

.....

Make a Firm Commitment to Personal Growth

Self-Improvement should be a motive an activity that we all should seek to apply to our lives. We can be comfortable with what we have obtained so far, and we can be comfortable with our condition or station in life as it is right now. However, when we look at the concept of life it is based on growth and development, it is based on Change.

As we move throughout life and go through calendar after calendar, we are literally in a continuously state of change. And even though this is a physical change, our mental and spiritual should grow and develop or change along with it.

Self-improvement covers our physical mental and spiritual bodies. With the science and activities of this book, we should be empowered to grow and develop exactly as we want. Self-improvement is just what it implies in its name. It's you improving yourself.

No one can tell you when you have achieved self-improvement and the only thing another person can do is to help you give you the tools that you need to be successful.

Self improvement is the equivalent of change. Change is an action word, meaning that you are in a state of movement or moving from one please or condition to another.

as we are looking at the word improvement, this is the frequency that we are tuned into, meaning that this action is based on a positive energy resulting in a positive effect on you.

Creating Me!

Since we know that our first concepts and ideas about ourselves comes from other people's perspectives of us, it is important for us to enter into the action of self-improvement with the goal being to create ourselves using our own concepts and ideas.

This is where many people get stuck or lost on/to themselves at - which is the concepts and ideas that we have from others. This doesn't have to be necessarily bad, but we have to understand that it is still other people's concepts and ideas about us.

These other people ideas and concepts are not based on our Power, they are not based on our Perfection, they are not based on our Life. These concepts and ideas are based on those people's ideas of power, perfection and life being projected on us.

Now it is your turn to create your own ideas and concepts about yourself and enter into the action of your improvement.

Self-improvement begins with Self-Concept.

The first principle for changing self-concept is the most difficult and the most important. You must make a firm commitment to cultivating personal growth. This isn't as easy as it might sound.

	Actual Self	Ideal Self
Private Self	How I see myself	How I would like to see myself
Public (Social) Self	How others see me	How I would like others to see me

A firm commitment involves more than saying, "I want to be more open to others." Or "I want to be more open to myself." Saying these sentences is simple and the easiest part.

You have to invest **energy** and **effort** to bring about change. From the start, realize that changing how you think of yourself is a major project.

Changing how we see ourselves is a long-term process, so we can't let setbacks undermine our commitment to change. Apparently, consistency itself is comforting and we can draw the strength that we need from being consistent to the commitment of our change.

PAGE 49

Supreme Health & Fitness!   Knowledge Of Self Series Vol 5!

We know ourselves better than anyone else. So, if you realize in advance that you may struggle against change, you'll be prepared for the tension that accompanies personal growth. The better prepared you are the more successful you will be at controlling them.

Most failure can be found in a person knowing their struggles but not adequately preparing to encounter or overcome their overcome their known short-comings.

Gain and Use Knowledge to Support Personal Growth

Commitment alone is insufficient to bring about constructive changes in your self- concept. In addition, you need several types of knowledge. First, you need to understand how your self-concept was formed.

Second, you need information about yourself. One way to get this information is through self-disclosure, which is revealing information about ourselves that others are unlikely to discover on their own.

Self-disclosure is an important way to learn about ourselves (Greene, Derlega, & Mathews, 2006). As we reveal our hopes, fears, dreams, and feelings, we get responses from others that give us new perspectives on who we are. This enables us to understand HOW our own Mind works in a given situation.

The Johari Window

	Known to self	Not known to self
Known to others	Open	Blind
Not known to others	Hidden	Unknown

In addition, we gain insight into ourselves by seeing how we interact with others in new situations which allows us to have more or better control over our interactions so that we can get the most from them.

A number of years ago, Joseph Luft and Harry Ingham (Luft, 1969) created a model of different sorts of knowledge that affect self-development.

PAGE 50

Supreme Health & Fitness!   Knowledge Of Self Series Vol 5!

Creating Me!

They called the model the Johari Window, which is a combination of their first names, Joe and Harry.

Four types of information are relevant to the self:

1. *Open*, or *public*, information is known both to us and to others. Your name, height, major, and tastes in music probably are open information that you share easily with others.

2. The *blind area* contains information that others know about us but we don't know about ourselves. For example, others may see that we are insecure even though we think we've hidden that well. Others may also recognize needs or feelings that we haven't acknowledged to ourselves.

3. *Hidden information* is what we know about ourselves but choose not to reveal to most others. You might not tell many people about your vulnerabilities or about traumas in your past because you consider this private information. The unknown area is made up of information about ourselves that neither we nor others know. This consists of your untapped resources, your untried talents, and your reactions to experiences you've never had. You don't know how you will manage a crisis until you've been in one, and you can't tell what kind of parent you would be unless you've had a child.

4. The *unknown area* is made up of information about ourselves that neither we nor others know. This consists of your untapped resources, your untried talents, and your reactions to experiences you've never had. You don't know how you will manage a crisis until you've been in one, and you can't tell what kind of parent you would be unless you've had a child.

	Known to self	Not known to self
Known to Others	The areas of your life that are the so-called open book.	The blind spots — we all have them.
Not Known to Others	The things you know about yourself but will not share with others.	The things about you that no one knows, not even you.

PAGE 51

Supreme Health & Fitness!   Knowledge Of Self Series Vol 5!

Set Goals That Are Realistic and Fair

This can be considered the most important aspect of developing your self-concept and oft-times is the catalyst between someone's failure or Success of creating their own self-concept. We set a goal for ourselves that is unobtainable which almost ensures our failure.

Efforts to change how we see ourselves work best when we set realistic and fair goals.

In a culture that emphasizes perfectionism, it's easy to be trapped into expecting more than is humanly possible.

Western society urges us to expect more and more of ourselves—more promotions and raises, more productivity, more possessions, more everything (Lacher, 2005). This type of mind-set creates an overly competitive environment that fosters an every-man-for-themselves attitude which is not conducive to Peace, Cooperation or Unity.

Peter Whybrow, who is the director of a neuroscience center, believes that Americans relentlessly seek possessions and status. He argues that the American addiction to having more of everything is futile because more is never enough; if we get more, we want even more! This is unrealistic and can only make us unhappy, because we can never achieve or have or be enough.

S	• **Specific:** State exactly what you want to accomplish (Who, What, Where, Why)
M	• **Measurable:** How will you demonstrate and evaluate the extent to which the goal has been met?
A	• **Achievable:** stretch and challenging goals within ability to achieve outcome. What is the action-oriented verb?
R	• **Relevant:** How does the goal tie into your key responsibilities? How is it aligned to objectives?
T	• **Time-bound:** Set 1 or more target dates, the "by when" to guide your goal to successful and timely completion (include deadlines, dates and frequency)

We should be fair to ourselves by acknowledging our strengths and virtues as well as our limitations and aspects of our- selves we want to change.

Creating Me!

Being fair to yourself also requires you to accept that you are **in process**. One across-the-board characteristic of the human self is that it is continually in process, always becoming. This implies several things.

Statement	Strongly Agree	Agree	Disagree	Strongly Disagree
1. I feel that I am a person of worth, at least on an equal plan with others.				
2. I feel that I have a number of good qualities.				
3. All in all, I am inclined to feel that I am a failure.				
4. I am able to do things as well as most other people				
5. I feel I do not have much to be proud of.				
6. I take a positive attitude toward myself.				
7. On the whole, I am satisfied with myself.				
8. I wish I could have more respect for myself				
9. I certainly feel useless at times.				
10. At times, I think I am no good at all.				

First, it means you need to accept who you are now as a starting point. You don't have to like or admire everything about yourself, but it is important to accept who you are now as a basis for going forward.

The self that you are results from all the interactions, reflected appraisals, and social comparisons you have made during your life, which was beyond our control. Once we accept this as who we are NOW, we can easily re-define ourselves according to our own definitions.

You cannot change your past, but you do not have to let it define your future.

Accepting yourself as in-process also implies that you realize you can change. Who you are is not who you will be in 5 or 10 years. Don't let yourself be hindered by defeating, self-fulfilling prophecies or the false idea that you cannot change (Rusk & Rusk, 1988).

You can *easily* change if you set realistic goals, make a genuine commitment, and then work for the changes you want.

According to psychiatrist Judith Orloff (2009), we are not generous with ourselves when it comes to compassion. Orloff says that many people are not self-compassionate because they think it's the same as being self-indulgent.

We render ourselves weak and powerless by allowing negative based ideas and beliefs from others to influence how we think of ourselves and treat ourselves. Everyone has a God-Given RIGHT to be able to DEFINE themselves and to live their life according to HOW they want.

Seek Contexts That Support Personal Change

Just as it is easier to swim with the tide than against it, it is easier to change our views of ourselves when we have some support for our efforts. You can do a lot to create an environment that supports your growth by choosing contexts and people who help you realize your goals.

First, think about settings. Example - If you want to become more extroverted, put yourself in social situations rather than in libraries.

Second, think about the people whose appraisals of you will help you move toward changes you desire. You can put yourself in supportive contexts by consciously choosing to be around people who believe in you and encourage your personal growth.

It's equally important to steer clear of people who pull us down or say we can't change. In other words, people who reflect positive appraisals of us enhance our ability to improve.

 One of the most crippling kinds of self-talk we can engage in is self-sabotage. This involves telling ourselves we are no good, we can't do something, there's no point in trying to change, and so forth. We may be repeating judgments others have made of us, or we may be inventing our own negative self-fulfilling prophecies. Either way, self-sabotage defeats us because it undermines belief in ourselves.

Self- sabotage is poisonous; it destroys our motivation to change and grow.

Creating Me!

We can also affirm our strengths, encourage our growth, and fortify our sense of self-worth. Positive self-talk builds motivation and belief in yourself.

It is also a useful strategy to interrupt and challenge negative messages from yourself and others.

The next time you hear yourself saying, "I can't do this" or someone else says, "You'll never change," challenge the negative message with self-talk. Say out loud to yourself, "I can do it. I will change."

Use positive self-talk to resist counterproductive communication about yourself. This creates the environment of Power IN You. Instead of wondering if you can accomplish something – YOU KNOW YOU CAN!

How true are these statements of you?	Slightly	Partly	Fairly	Mostly	Totally
I am beginning to question whether my negative picture of myself is really accurate					
I don't get so anxious or upset when I think about who I am and what I am like					
I am feeling more optimistic about what I can do in the future					
I feel more confident and relaxed generally					
I am really looking forward to making positive changes for myself					

PAGE 55

Supreme Health & Fitness!   Knowledge Of Self Series Vol 5!

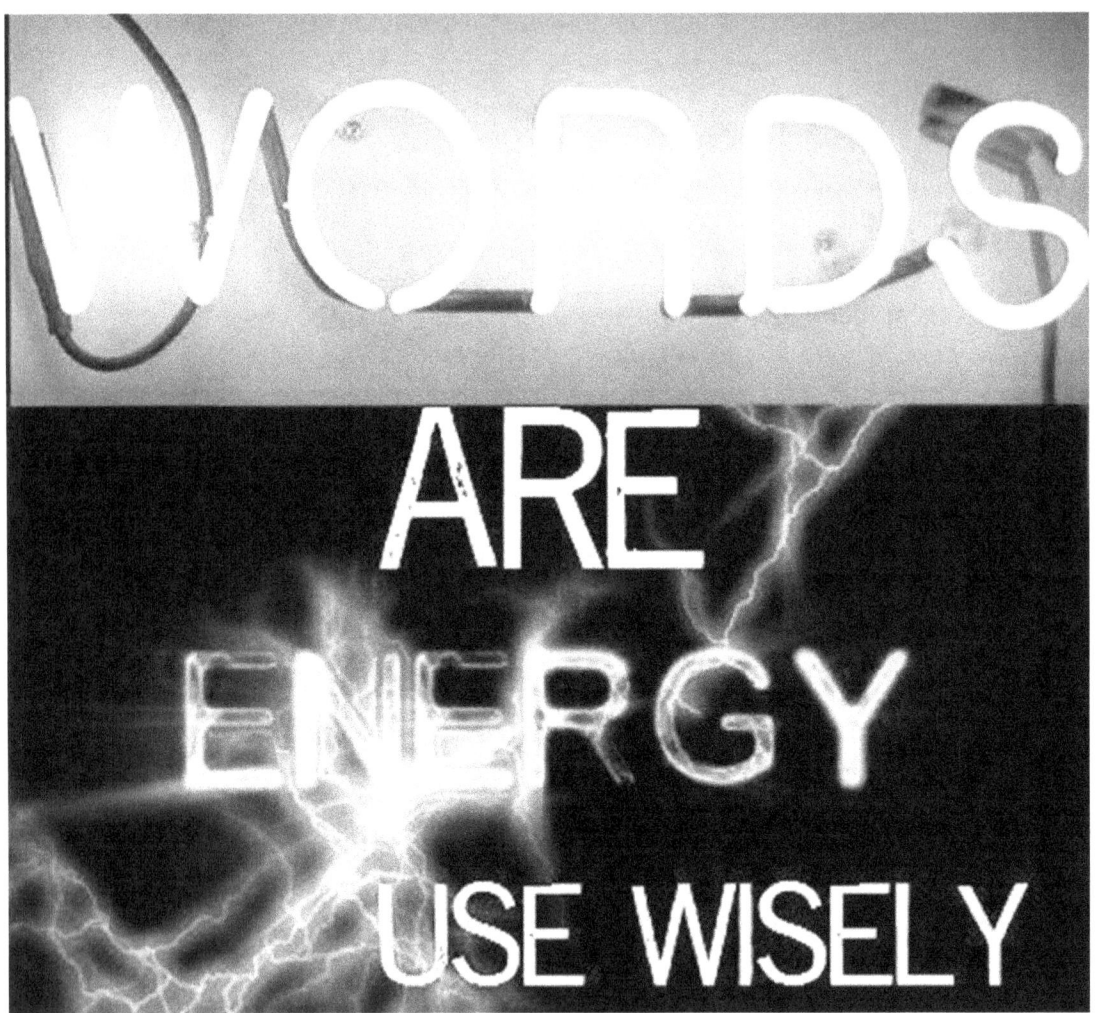

PAGE 56

Supreme Health & Fitness!   Knowledge Of Self Series Vol 5!

The Power of Self-Compassion

How often are we actually grateful to ourselves?
When we take note of our positive qualities, and celebrate our
lives and ourselves, we become not only happier,
but more successful. It helps to see yourself as you really are.
Even if you see real weakness, addressing them from a place
of self-compassion will help you thrive. Here are some tips
for how to make self-compassion a habit:

Notice Your Self-Talk

In times of failure or challenge, noticing your self-talk can
help you replace it with self-compassion. Instead of saying
things like "I'm such an idiot!" you might say "I had a moment
of absentmindedness and that's okay."

Write Yourself a Letter

When your emotions are overhwhelming, write a letter to
yourself as if you were writing to a friend. It might feel strange
at first, but your comforting words will help to normalize the
situation rather than blow it out of proportion.

Develop a Self-Compassion Phrase

Use a mantra or a phrase that you can turn to in challenging
situations, so you can deal with them calmly and with grace.
Dr. Kristin Neff, a self-compassion researcher, uses the mantra
"This is a moment of suffering. Suffering is part of life. May
I be kind to myself in this moment; may I give myself the
compassion I need."

Make a Daily Gratitude List

Write down 5 things you feel grateful for every day, or are
proud of having accomplished. This may sound overly
simplistic, but this extremely short exercise can produce
powerful and long-lasting results.

Self-Esteem Journal

MON.	Something I did well today...	
	Today I had fun when...	
	I felt proud when...	
TUE.	Today I accomplished...	
	I had a positive experience with...	
	Something I did for someone...	
WED.	I felt good about myself when...	
	I was proud of someone else...	
	Today was interesting because...	
THUR.	I felt proud when...	
	A positive thing I witnessed...	
	Today I accomplished...	
FRI.	Something I did well today...	
	I had a positive experience with (a person, place, or thing)...	
	I was proud of someone when...	
SAT.	Today I had fun when...	
	Something I did for someone...	
	I felt good about myself when...	
SUN.	A positive thing I witnessed...	
	Today was interesting because...	
	I felt proud when...	

Positive Experiences

Write briefly about times when you displayed each of the following qualities.

_____

Courage

_____

Kindness

_____

Selflessness

_____

Love

_____

Sacrifice

_____

Wisdom

_____

Happiness

_____

Determination

PAGE 59

Supreme Health & Fitness!   Knowledge Of Self Series Vol 5!

daily Self love Worksheets

I **LOVE** MYSELF TODAY BECAUSE ...

TODAY I FORGIVE MYSELF THAT ...

I AM _____ BECAUSE ...

SOMETHING GOOD I DID FOR MYSELF TODAY

NOTES

I **LOVE** MYSELF TODAY BECAUSE ...

TODAY I FORGIVE MYSELF THAT ...

I AM _____ BECAUSE ...

SOMETHING GOOD I DID FOR MYSELF TODAY

NOTES

PAGE 60

Supreme Health & Fitness!   Knowledge Of Self Series Vol 5!

Test Your Emotional Intelligence

This is a list of situations each followed by five possible responses (ALWAYS, USUALLY, SOMETIMES, RARELY AND NEVER).

Read each sentence carefully and out of the five possible responses, choose the one which seems to you to be the most appropriate response for a particular situation.

Always: A/ Usually: U/ Sometimes: S/ Rarely: R/ Never: N.

S.No.		A	U	S	R	N
1-	I extend help to anyone who is in need without expecting any return.					
2-	I am very sensitive and respective to the feelings of others.					
3-	I do not allow my emotions to spell to spoil my relations with others. I am always in control of my emotions.					
4-	If someone harms me in any way. I do not forget it easily; I am on a lookout to retaliate in the same coin.					
5-	I never have problem adjusting with any kind of person.					
6-	I feel guilty for any wrong that I may have done in the past.					
7-	I try to share others grief or turmoil, I am sympathetic and caring when someone is in pain.					
8-	Between the two, I get more happiness and peace of mind in giving rather than taking.					
9-	I solve a problem as soon as I confront it, and it keeps me free from worries.					
10-	I look at my problem with an open mind. I never allow my feelings and emotions to highjack my decisions and actions.					
11-	My feelings are one with the suffering person. I try to spend time with that person and share his grief and sorrow.					

PAGE 61

Supreme Health & Fitness!   Knowledge Of Self Series Vol 5!

12-	Certain situations and some people evoke revulsion in me.					
13-	I get hurt very easily. On such occasions I feel humiliated and degraded.					
14-	I cannot express myself fully before others. I am generally inhibited in my behaviour.					
15-	Emotionally, I am bland. I do not get disturbed even at the suffering of my near and dear ones.					
16-	I set realistic goals and pursue them with tenacity.					
17-	I have good insight into my thinking and actions and I am in complete control of my behaviour.					
18-	I never react when I am angry. I analyse each situation thoroughly when I am cool and then react.					
19-	For me two plus two is always five. I am optimistic even in face of repeated failure.					
20-	I have a positive attitude in life. I always help people whenever I can. I do not work against the interest of anyone.					

PAGE 62

Supreme Health & Fitness!   Knowledge Of Self Series Vol 5!

SELF-TALK WORKSHEET
Changing From Negative to Positive

In many situations, the only thing we can control is our own response. Changing self-talk from negative to positive is an excellent way to manage that response and stress.

Naming

We all name our experiences. "Crisis," "bad as usual," "a great challenge" are names you might give to things that happen.

Pick a recent upsetting experience. Describe it in a few words.

Is there a positive name you could give it? (learning experience, chance to change, etc.)

List the names you gave to five recent experiences, good or bad.

If they happened to someone else, what other positive names could you give them?

Letting Go

You often must let go of dreams, people or parts of your life. Letting go allows you to get on with your life when something is over.

Write down two things you need to let go of.

Imagine that each one is really going out of your life. How do you feel? (sad, angry, relieved, etc)

Who can you tell about your feeling?

What advice would you give to someone who is in your situation?

Belief and Faith

Self-talk reflects our belief in who we are or in the universe. A positive faith can help you during stressful times.

Name 10 positive things you believe in about yourself people or the universe. If you can't think of 10 beliefs, ask other people for theirs.

Describe a recent experience and how you used one of these beliefs to help you.

IMPROVE THE MOMENT WORKSHEET
ADVANCED DISTRESS TOLERANCE SKILLS

IMAGERY

1. WHEN RUMINATING ABOUT THE PAST
a. Remember & LIST times/things you did you're proud of or at which you were successful.

  - _____

  - _____

  - _____

b. Remember & LIST any good memories or people from your past who were kind/helpful.

  - _____

  - _____

  - _____

c. Safe Place (describe) _____

  _____

FLASHBACKS
a. When having flashbacks, imagine each memory:
  - being encased in a balloon and, when you pop the balloon, the flashback explodes.
  - being encased in a piñata. When you break the piñata, what will come out of it?

  _____

b. When having flashbacks:
  1. Imagine yourself shrinking the images and memories that come into your head and then picking them up and putting them in a tiny box & burning it or in a bottle.
  2. Imagine changing the colors in the images to black & white.
  3. Imagine making the images out of focus or turning them upside down.
  4. Imagine turning the volume down or increasing the speed to chipmunk speed.

c. When having flashbacks:
  - Imagine yourself surrounded by the police, army, or whatever forces you need to be in control of this memory and make things happen in your imagination the way you wished it could have happened years ago. Who would you bring with you & what would they do?

  _____

  _____

  _____

2. WHEN RUMINATING ABOUT THE FUTURE
a. Play the positive "What if…" Game and imagine good things happening.
  - What if _____ [something good] happened?
  - What if _____ [everything turned out better than I hoped]?
  - Ask what am I able to do now? What is needed? Let go of the impossible.

b. IMAGINE (Yourself as a superhero able to "save the day" and vanquish all the bad guys).
  - What super powers would you have? _____.
  - What would your "Super" name be? _____.
  - What kind of costume would you wear? _____.

c. What if you over-extended your catastrophizing & imagined adding lots of silly things to the story your mind is trying to tell you?

d. What if your wildest & best fantasy came true? What would happen?

PAGE 64

Supreme Health & Fitness!   Knowledge Of Self Series Vol 5!

5 THINGS THAT I LIKE ABOUT MYSELF...

1) _____

2) _____

3) _____

4) _____

5) _____

daily Self love Worksheets

I LOVE MYSELF TODAY BECAUSE

TODAY I FORGIVE MYSELF THAT

I AM _____ BECAUSE

SOMETHING GOOD I DID FOR MYSELF TODAY

NOTES

I LOVE MYSELF TODAY BECAUSE

TODAY I FORGIVE MYSELF THAT

I AM _____ BECAUSE

SOMETHING GOOD I DID FOR MYSELF TODAY

NOTES

PAGE 66

Supreme Health & Fitness!   Knowledge Of Self Series Vol 5!

self REFLECTION
WORKSHEET

IMPORTANT CONVERSATION YOU WILL EVER HAVE IS HAVE with YOURSELF

Things I am good at

1. _____
2. _____
3. _____
4. _____
5. _____

What I am passionate about

_____
_____

What I love most about ME

_____
_____
_____

Ways I can live my passion

_____
_____
_____
_____
_____

Quotes that inspires ME

_____
_____
_____

PAGE 67

Supreme Health & Fitness!   Knowledge Of Self Series Vol 5!

"Today is an incredible day! Success, Prosperity, and Abundance, in many different forms have naturally found their way into my life today. I gratefully enjoy their manifestations throughout my day and happily share these blessings of abundance with many others in order to bring happiness to their day as well."

"I Am Happy"
"I Am Healthy"
"I Am Wealthy"
"I Am Secure"
"I Am Worthy"
"I Am Positive"
"I Am Blessed"
"I Am Grateful"
"I Am Beautiful"
"I Am Confident"
"I Am Courageous"
"I Am Excited About Today
"I Am Loved"

Physical Self-Care
Nutrition
Sleep
Exercise
Water intake
Medication
Supplements
Breathing

Spiritual Self-Care
Prayer
Meditation
Spiritual community
Forgiveness
Finding purpose
and meaning

The Goal
To feel
vital and balanced,
free from depression
and anxiety

Lifestyle
Structure/routine
Relaxation
Setting goals
Fulfilling work
Time in nature
Pleasure

Mental/Emotional
Self-Care
Positive self talk
Positive beliefs
Feeling one's feelings
Mood journal
A library of positive memories
Psychotherapy
Family of origin healing
Working through grief
Working with a good therapist

People Support
Family
Friends
Psychiatrist/therapist
Minster/rabbi
Support group
Day treatment
Community service

PAGE 69

Supreme Health & Fitness!   Knowledge Of Self Series Vol 5!

WORDS WILL MANIFEST!

Chapter Three

Creating Me!

* * * * *

Did you know one positive word can change water's structure? Do you know that there is proof. A Japanese scientist named Masaru Emoto made a series of tests and discovered some very interesting results.

Emoto realized both positive and negative words can have an influence on water's structure by changing water's crystals.

During his study of water, Emoto came to some fascinating revelations. He came to a belief that water was the so-called ''blueprint of our reality'' and our emotional energy and vibrations can change the physical structure of water. Emoto's tests mostly consisted of putting water in glasses and then exposing it to different words, pictures, and music and then freezing it and analyzing how water crystals look. And through his research and analysis, he came to the conclusion that if we "influence" water with positive words, pictures, or music that water crystals will be nicely formed.

On the other hand, if one puts water near negative influences, such as saying negative words, or if you turn on some loud heavy metal music then the results would be the total opposite.

Those water crystals will be distorted and formed in an ugly and negative formation.

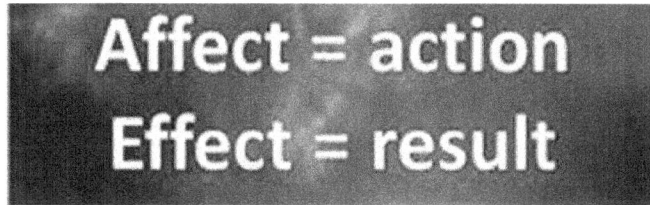

Creating Me!

But what happens with us when we are influenced by both positive and negative things? Do we react the same way water reacts? Does our molecule structure also change when someone says something nice to us?

The answer for that is simply — yes.

We are approximately 75% WATER and as such we are also prone to changes. Our molecule structure also changes when influenced by different words, music, movies, scenes of violence (or love), etc…... Water Absorbs and is SHAPED by its outside environment and Energy.

Words are Energy or Contain Energy ….. When we Hear Words – from ourselves or others – the Energy Shapes and Affects US – Transforming YOU INTO THOSE WORDS/ENERGY!

You will use this Science to AFFECT and EFFECT Your Healing, Life, Power and Greatness!!!

MESSAGES FROM WATER

How the molecular structure of water is affected...

Mr. Emoto's
- human, thoughts, words, ideas and music, affect the molecular structure of water,
- 70% of our human body is water
- 70% covers of our planet

Original water

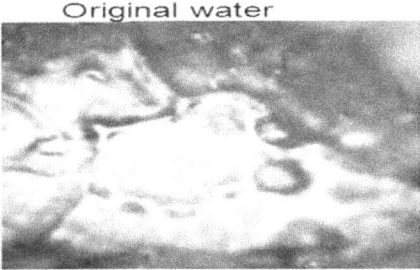

Water after Prayer

With this WorkBook, You are creating Your Own High Energy Words and Language, that when you Read and Hear them You Shape Yourself INTO them.

You Write and Read the High Energy Words of YOUR HEALING = Shape and Affect YOUR HEALING!

PAGE 72

Supreme Health & Fitness!   Knowledge Of Self Series Vol 5!

Creating Me!

You will create the AFFECT of the Action of Energy that will Successfully EFFECT and make Manifest YOUR HEALING!

Positive Message
Positive words and energies(vibrations) form beautiful crystals.

Love	Angel	Please,
After praying	Cosmos	Sun
spring	summer	fall
winter	Arirang (Korea song)	Mozart (music)
Thank you	고맙습니다 (Korea)	Grazie (Italy)
Danke (German)	Merci (France)	謝謝 (China)

Thank you

With this book, you will apply the Science of words and sounds on Water to Positively Vibrate and raise the Energy Level and Frequency of Your Water of Your Body.

By Thinking Positive High Energy words, the Foundation is laid for your Transformation INTO your Thoughts. These Thoughts create the Energy and Vibration level in you.

You reinforce and increase this energy and vibration by WRITING down your Thoughts. This is ACTION and involves You moving the Water of Your Body to physically manifest your unseen Thought.

After the Action of WRITING, now you take the Empowering Action of READING your Thoughts. The Act of Reading creates vibrations and energy IN you to is attuned to the Words you are reading. Because these are HIGH Energy words, written about Your HEALING, Life, Power and Greatness – Your further increasing the CHANGE of yourself INTO your Words.

PAGE 73

Supreme Health & Fitness!   Knowledge Of Self Series Vol 5!

Creating Me!

This means you are transforming the Thought of Healing INTO the ACTION of Healing!

Dr. Emoto tested water samples by writing and focusing negative words, thoughts and intentions on one set, and positive, loving intentions on the other. The results showed that bad thoughts provided ugly, unappealing water crystals. Happy thoughts in turn, created beautiful, intricate water crystals.

EVERY Word you HEAR is a form of VIBRATION.

The Act of Listening is your Eardrum interpreting the Energy or Sound that you Hear OUTSIDE of you into Energy and Vibration INSIDE YOU!

This Shapes the Water of your Body INTO the Words that you Hear.

You are beginning the Process of re-defining yourself and creating your own definitions of Self while simultaneously creating the environment IN Self that allows You To HEAL YOURSELF!

You are using this science to increase the Quality of Your LIFE!

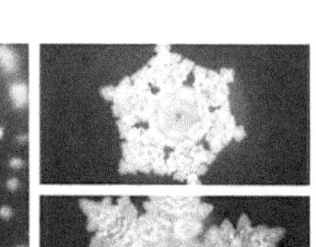

You are applying this science to make manifest Your POWER!

Its already IN YOU ….. with this book, you will create the Words for Your Own Story of Healing, Health, Life, Power and Greatness!!!

If a person is positive, cheerful and optimistic, it can change how other persons around him or she will feel. That person can, just by being close to others, spread positive energy.

There are many real-life proofs that being positive (just like negativity) spreads and it's the same with positive and negative words (words of gratitude, affection, complimenting words), music and songs that spread positivity, even nice pictures.

The water in us reacts to those positive things and because of that, we need to say positive words to ourselves on a constant and consistent basis. Your positive words will not only make you feel better, they will Shape You INTO them.

Understand that its not just the Word …. It's the Energy associated with the word.

Creating Me!

As you Think, Write, Speak and Listen to Your story of Healing, Health, Life, Power and Greatness, you create Vibration at every stage. The Strength and Power of the Vibration is a result of the particular word used.

ALL WATER ABSORBS, REACTS IS AFFECTED BY VIBRATION!!!!

In this case, YOU or more specifically YOUR WORDS are the Cause of the Vibrations......
which means YOU ARE SHAPING YOURSELF INTO YOUR OWN SELF!!!!!!

YOU CAN CAUSE YOUR OWN HEALING!!!!

YOU CAN EMPOWER YOURSELF!!!!!

YOU CAN SUCCESSFULLY ENJOY YOUR ABUNDANT LIFE!!!!

Thoughts and Words Affect Water

After seeing water react to different environmental conditions, pollution and music, Mr. Emoto and colleagues decided to see how thoughts and words affected the formation of untreated, distilled, water crystals, using words typed onto paper by a word processor and taped on glass bottles overnight.

The same procedure was performed using the names of deceased persons. The waters were then frozen and photographed.

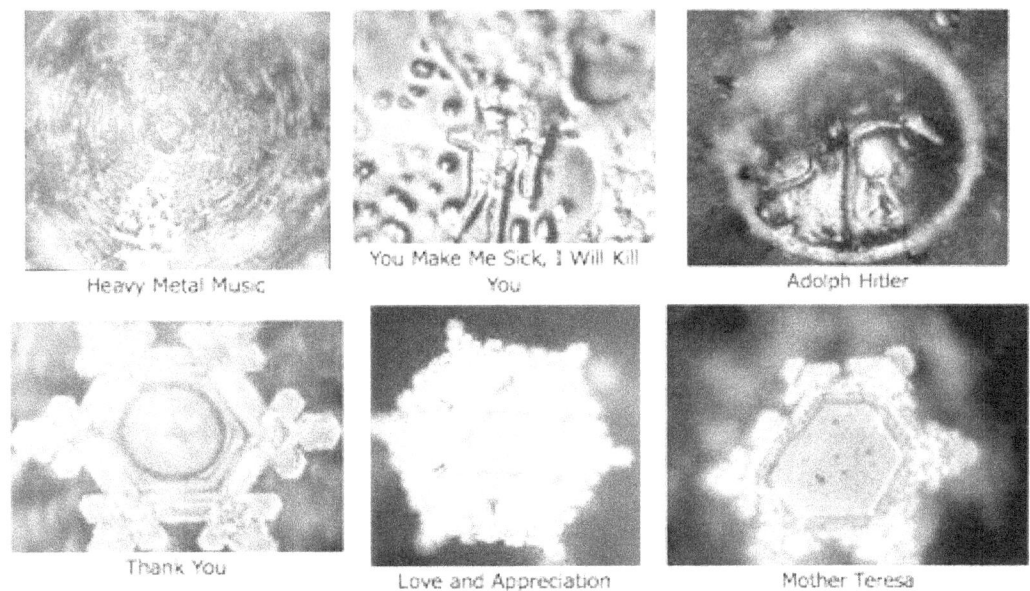

Heavy Metal Music

You Make Me Sick, I Will Kill You

Adolph Hitler

Thank You

Love and Appreciation

Mother Teresa

PAGE 75

Supreme Health & Fitness!   Knowledge Of Self Series Vol 5!

5 Daily Reminders

1. I am amazing.
2. I can do anything.
3. Positivity is a choice.
4. I celebrate my individuality.
5. I am prepared to succeed.

Time Management

Organising Your Time & Plan Your Day

It's not possible to *manage* time because time doesn't actually exist. It is possible to organise your daily activities and make better use of the time that's available during the day.

PLAN YOUR TOMORROW AT THE END OF YOUR TODAY.

- If you are at work – plan your next day before you leave the workplace.
- If you are at home – plan your next day before going to sleep at night.

Take some time at the end of your day to finish up loose ends and focus on the priorities for the next day. Plan what needs to get done without overloading your schedule. If you have really important tasks that HAVE to be done - delegate time just for them.

It's not enough to be busy. The question is: "What are you busy about?"

Consider these questions when organising your tomorrow:

- What tasks need to be done to move forward in your project/goal?
- What is the best order for them to be done in?
- What tasks need to be done first?
- Which ones would you choose to be done tomorrow? The next day? Next week? Next month? And so on.
- When considering the tasks that need to be done tomorrow: Have you got enough time in the day to accomplish these tasks?
- Are there any tasks that you can delegate to another person?
- Do you need more information about a task before it can be completed?
- Are you more alert and at optimal potential in the morning or the afternoon? (Delegate tasks accordingly).
- What jobs or tasks are you forgetting?

Supreme Health & Fitness!   Knowledge Of Self Series Vol 5!

PAGE 77

Creating Me!

Open To Create . . .

EMOTIONAL INTELLIGENCE: Personal Review

'Anyone can be angry - that is easy. But to be angry with the right person, to the right degrees at the right time, for the right purpose, and in the right way — that is not easy.' - **Aristotle**

Exercise: Consider the questions below and score yourself out of ten for each one (ten being high). Consider your responses and notice areas where you scored 'low'. These are your areas for potential growth and may also indicate your personal vulnerabilities and greatest challenges. Also, notice where you confidently scored 'high' - these areas have the potential to support your challenges.

Emotional Intelligence	Score 10	Notes to self
Emotional Management		
If you are sad, grieving or mourning, do you allow yourself to cry? Can you cry openly in front of others?		
Can you express anger freely and non-destructively and then let it go?		
Do you quickly let go of grudges and resentment?		
When you are afraid, do you let trusted others see your fear?		
Are you able to recognise when you need help, then ask for help or support?		
Can you receive help, as well as give it?		
Can you say 'no' without feeling guilty?		
Can you strongly protest against mistreatment of self or others?		
Do you easily express, as well as receive, tenderness, love, passion?		
Can you enjoy your own company yet gladly and comfortably accept intimacy?		
Do you listen clearly to yourself and to others?		
Can you empathise with the needs and feelings of others, without judgement or criticism?		
Can you motivate others without resorting to fear tactics or manipulation?		
Do you allow yourself to frequently experience and enjoy pleasure?		

PAGE 78

Supreme Health & Fitness!   Knowledge Of Self Series Vol 5!

Open To Create . . .

When necessary, can you contain (rather than repress) your impulses and delay your gratification, without resorting to guilt, shame, or suppression of your emotions?

Do you allow yourself to experience bliss, ecstasy, excitement, fascination and awe?

Do you often laugh out loud — a deep belly laugh?

Do you sometimes feel moved by the courage or the spirit of others?

Flexibility and balance

Can you focus your energy on work, yet balance this with fun and rest?

Can you accept and even enjoy others who have different needs and world-views?

Do you let yourself be spontaneous, play like a child, be silly?

Are your goals realistic, and does your patience allow you to work towards them steadily?

Self awareness and positive esteem

Can you forgive yourself your mistakes, and take yourself lightly?

Can you accept your own shortcomings, without feeling ashamed, and remain excited about learning and growing?

Do you respect your strengths and vulnerabilities, rather than inflate with pride, or fester with shame?

Would you say you are generally true to yourself without blindly rebelling against, nor conforming to social expectations?

Can you bear disappointment or frustration, without succumbing to criticism of self or others?

Are you kind to yourself, do you avoid being hard — even punishing towards yourself?

PAGE 79

Supreme Health & Fitness!   Knowledge Of Self Series Vol 5!

How to Build Confidence

Evaluate Your Confidence Levels

Statement	Strongly Agree	Agree	Neutral	Disagree	Strongly Disagree
I have a clear sense of what's important to me.					
I know what I want in life.					
I admit my mistakes and know that setbacks can be learned from.					
I can stand back and think clearly when things get emotional.					
Most of my work involves things I enjoy doing.					
I make other people feel good about themselves.					
People know me as being an optimistic.					
I respect myself and others.					
I am realistic about my strengths and weaknesses.					
I know what others consider to be my strengths.					
I freely ask for help.					
I am able to see the wider perspective and the smaller details of a situation.					
I enjoy taking on new challenges.					
I seek out opportunities to learn and grow					
I take care of my mind and body.					
I handle stress with ease and don't take things too personally.					
I am clear about my purpose in life.					
I have positive yet realistic expectations.					
Even though I dive in to new opportunities I have a balanced perspective about risk taking.					

PAGE 80

Supreme Health & Fitness!   Knowledge Of Self Series Vol 5!

Creating Me!

What my body does for me:

1. _____
2. _____
3. _____
4. _____
5. _____

What I love about my body:

1. _____
2. _____
3. _____
4. _____
5. _____

What's unique about me:

1. _____
2. _____
3. _____
4. _____
5. _____

What I can do to help it stay strong and healthy:

1. _____
2. _____
3. _____
4. _____
5. _____

About Me
Sentence Completion

I was really happy when... _____

_____

Something that my friends like about me is... _____

_____

I'm proud of... _____

_____

My family was happy when I... _____

_____

In school, I'm good at... _____

_____

Something that makes me unique is... _____

_____

PAGE 82

Supreme Health & Fitness!　　　　　　　　Knowledge Of Self Series Vol 5!

ALL ABOUT ME!

My favorite color is...	My favorite subject is...	I'm most happy when I...
The last movie I watched was...	My favorite food is...	I really hate it when...
Yesterday, I...	Most people don't know that I...	If I had a million dollars...
Tomorrow, I will...	Right now, I feel very...	My favorite memory is...

2 TRUTHS AND A LIE!

Write down two truthful statements and one lie! Have others guess which one they think is a lie.
Remember to make your lie something believable!

1. _____

2. _____

3. _____

PAGE 83

Supreme Health & Fitness!   Knowledge Of Self Series Vol 5!

"Develop your Emotional Intelligence !"

The following techniques and tips will enable you to progress at your own speed. They will provide you with food for thought for each of the test's eight themes, and help pave the way for your increased emotional independence

Self-knowledge

A   Identify difficulties to better deal with them (fatigue, stress, anxiety, etc.)
B   Differentiate between good stress, which energizes, and bad stress, which drains
C   Get to know your limits and learn to set yourself reachable goals
D   Listen to others

Self-control

A   Learn to take it easy, to relax. Stress can be neutralized very simply
B   Learn to build moments of rest into your day, and to better organize yourself
C   A sane mind in a sane body: maintain a healthy life style, eat a balanced diet and don't neglect sports!
D   Tips for conquering stress (or stage fright)
E   Learn to analyze your anger and to get a better grip on it

PAGE 84

Supreme Health & Fitness!   Knowledge Of Self Series Vol 5!

Creating Me!

Directions: Each of the following items asks you about your emotions or reactions associated with emotions. After deciding whether a statement is generally true for you, use the 5-point scale to respond to the statement. Please circle the "1" if you strongly disagree that this is like you, the "2" if you somewhat disagree that this is like you, "3" if you neither agree nor disagree that this is like you, the "4" if you somewhat agree that this is like you, and the "5" if you strongly agree that this is like you.

There are no right or wrong answers. Please give the response that best describes you.

1 = strongly disagree
2 = somewhat disagree
3 = neither agree nor disagree
4 = somewhat agree
5 = strongly agree

1.	I know when to speak about my personal problems to others.	1	2	3	4	5
2.	When I am faced with obstacles, I remember times I faced similar obstacles and overcame them.	1	2	3	4	5
3.	I expect that I will do well on most things I try.	1	2	3	4	5
4.	Other people find it easy to confide in me.	1	2	3	4	5
5.	I find it hard to understand the non-verbal messages of other people.	1	2	3	4	5
6.	Some of the major events of my life have led me to re-evaluate what is important and not important.	1	2	3	4	5
7.	When my mood changes, I see new possibilities.	1	2	3	4	5
8.	Emotions are one of the things that make my life worth living.	1	2	3	4	5
9.	I am aware of my emotions as I experience them.	1	2	3	4	5
10.	I expect good things to happen.	1	2	3	4	5
11.	I like to share my emotions with others.	1	2	3	4	5
12.	When I experience a positive emotion, I know how to make it last.	1	2	3	4	5
13.	I arrange events others enjoy.	1	2	3	4	5
14.	I seek out activities that make me happy.	1	2	3	4	5
15.	I am aware of the non-verbal messages I send to others.	1	2	3	4	5

PAGE 85

Supreme Health & Fitness!　　　　　Knowledge Of Self Series Vol 5!

How to Build Confidence

Evaluate Your Confidence Levels

Statement	Strongly Agree	Agree	Neutral	Disagree	Strongly Disagree
I have a clear sense of what's important to me.					
I know what I want in life.					
I admit my mistakes and know that setbacks can be learned from.					
I can stand back and think clearly when things get emotional.					
Most of my work involves things I enjoy doing.					
I make other people feel good about themselves.					
People know me as being an optimistic.					
I respect myself and others.					
I am realistic about my strengths and weaknesses.					
I know what others consider to be my strengths.					
I freely ask for help.					
I am able to see the wider perspective and the smaller details of a situation.					
I enjoy taking on new challenges.					
I seek out opportunities to learn and grow.					
I take care of my mind and body.					
I handle stress with ease and don't take things too personally.					
I am clear about my purpose in life.					
I have positive yet realistic expectations.					
Even though I dive in to new opportunities I have a balanced perspective about risk taking.					

PAGE 86

Supreme Health & Fitness!   Knowledge Of Self Series Vol 5!

Creating Me!

Challenging Negative Thoughts

Automatic negative thoughts (ANTs) only have power to affect our mood and lives if we let them. Sometimes ANTs can make things seem like a bigger deal than they really are, and those negative thoughts can affect the way you perceive and react to the situation. It is important to know how to control ANTs so they do not control you. Next time you feel a negative emotion and feel yourself about to react, consider these questions:

What happened?

_____

_____

Why is this upsetting?

_____

_____

What is the negative thought? How does it make you feel?

_____

_____

How does what happened affect the next 5 minutes? 24 hours? 7 days?

_____

_____

How does what happened affect your quality of life?

_____

_____

How much power are you giving the negative thought?

_____

_____

Does that negative thought deserve the control it has over you?

_____

_____

Next time you have this negative thought, what will you remind yourself to stay in control?

_____

_____

PAGE 87

Supreme Health & Fitness!　　　　　Knowledge Of Self Series Vol 5!

BAD HABITS THAT SHOW LACK OF SELF-ESTEEM

1. Saying "yes" to everything
2. Negative self-talk or self-criticism
3. Back down when opinions are challenged by others
4. Being indecisive with simple decisions
5. Fearing failure
6. Taking constructive criticism personally
7. Sweating the small stuff
8. Afraid to share your opinions in a conversation
9. Giving up too easily
10. Comparing yourself negatively to others
11. Slouching
12. Fidgeting
13. Claiming your successes are just luck
14. Buying things because others like them, not because you like them
15. Social withdrawal
16. Excessive preoccupation with personal problems
17. Letting fear stop you from trying new things

PAGE 88

Supreme Health & Fitness!   Knowledge Of Self Series Vol 5!

Behavioral Activation

You can begin to decrease depression by engaging in activities you find enjoyable, and by taking care of responsibilities that you have been neglecting

List three activities you enjoy:

1.

2.

3.

List three responsibilities you need to take care of:

1.

2.

3.

Try doing at least one activity or responsibility each day. Use the following scale to rate your depression, pleasant feelings, and sense of achievement before and after the activity

0	1	2	3	4	5	6	7	8
None	Minimal	Slight	Mild	Moderate	A Lot	Higher	Very High	Extreme

Activity (location, date, time)		Depression	Pleasure	Achievement
	Before			
	After			
	Before			
	After			
	Before			
	After			

Supreme Health & Fitness!　　　　　　　　Knowledge Of Self Series Vol 5!

PAGE 89

The Not-To-Do List

EVERYTHING ON MY PLATE

OTHER PEOPLE'S RESPONSIBILITIES

STUFF THAT'S OUT OF MY CONTROL

STUFF THAT DRAINS ME

STUFF THAT DOESN'T NEED TO GET DONE

Creating Me!

Stress Management
Self-Care Checklist

On a scale of 1 to 10, rank the level of stress you feel right now:

| | | | | | | | | | |
|1|2|3|4|5|6|7|8|9|10|

What is the biggest source of stress in your life today?

○ **Work**

Is there a clear separation between work and home? Are you frustrated with your colleagues or boss? Are the expectations at work set impossibly high?

○ **Family**

Is there division in your family? Are you having a difficult time adjusting to family changes? Is there a lack of communication between parents, siblings, partners, or kids?

○ **Conflict**

Are there any unresolved conflicts in your life right now? Are there recurring disagreements at work or with loved ones? Are both sides willing to achieve a peaceful resolution?

○ **Money**

Is money causing tension in your relationships? Are you finding it difficult to pay the bills and provide a quality life for your family? Are you having a difficult time agreeing on a financial plan or budget?

○ **Illness**

Are you (or someone you love) suffering from disease, illness or a loss of a loved one? Are you having a difficult time concentrating or completing day-to-day tasks due to an illness? Are you getting the medical care and attention you need and deserve?

○ **Other**

Are you having a difficult time articulating your thoughts and feelings? Are you seeking to control an uncontrollable situation? Are you able to minimize stress by planning and organizing ahead of time?

PAGE 91

Supreme Health & Fitness!　　　　Knowledge Of Self Series Vol 5!

Stress Diary
Finding Your Optimum Stress Levels:

Keeping a stress diary is an effective way of finding out what causes you stress, the level of stress you can handle and how you cope with stressors.

In your diary, write down your stress levels and how you feel throughout the day. In particular, notice "stressful" events. Record the following information:

- At least 5 times a day (on the hour - the same every day) write down:

  - The time
  - The amount of stress that you feel (on a scale of 1 to 10)
  - The emotions you are experiencing
  - How efficiently you think you are accomplishing things

- When you are feeling "stressed", write down:
  - Briefly describe the situation.
  - When and where did it occur?
  - What important factors made the event stressful?
  - Rate how stressful it was, on a scale of 1 to 10.
  - How did you handle the event?
  - Do you feel you handled the event well?
  - Did you deal with the cause or the symptom?
  - Overall, do you feel that you dealt with the stressor effectively?

THE ULTIMATE
guide to
Self-Compassion

Three Elements of Self-compassion

1. Self-kindness

"What I'm going through is very hard right now."

2. Common Humanity

"What I'm going through is hard, but I'm not alone. Everybody goes through adversity."

3. Mindfulness

"I am here and I see you."

Self-compassion IS NOT:	VS	Self-compassion IS :
Selfishness & Narcissism		Self-compassion quiets down the ego and minimizes the egoistic sense of self without ignoring or suppressing the self's needs
Judgment & Criticism		Having a kind understanding and an open mind, and acceptance.
Self-pity		Self-compassion allows us to step back and take the approach of other towards oneself.
Self-indulgence		Caring awareness which allows us to listen to our bodies and find out what is healthy for us.

Benefits of Self-compassion

Motivation and self-improvement

Eudaimonic happiness

Lowered symptoms of depression

How to put self-compassion into practice

Cultivate mindfulness

Cultivate forgiveness towards self

Hug yourself and speak to yourself softly

Write a letter to yourself from a perspective of unconditional acceptance

Practice loving kindness meditation

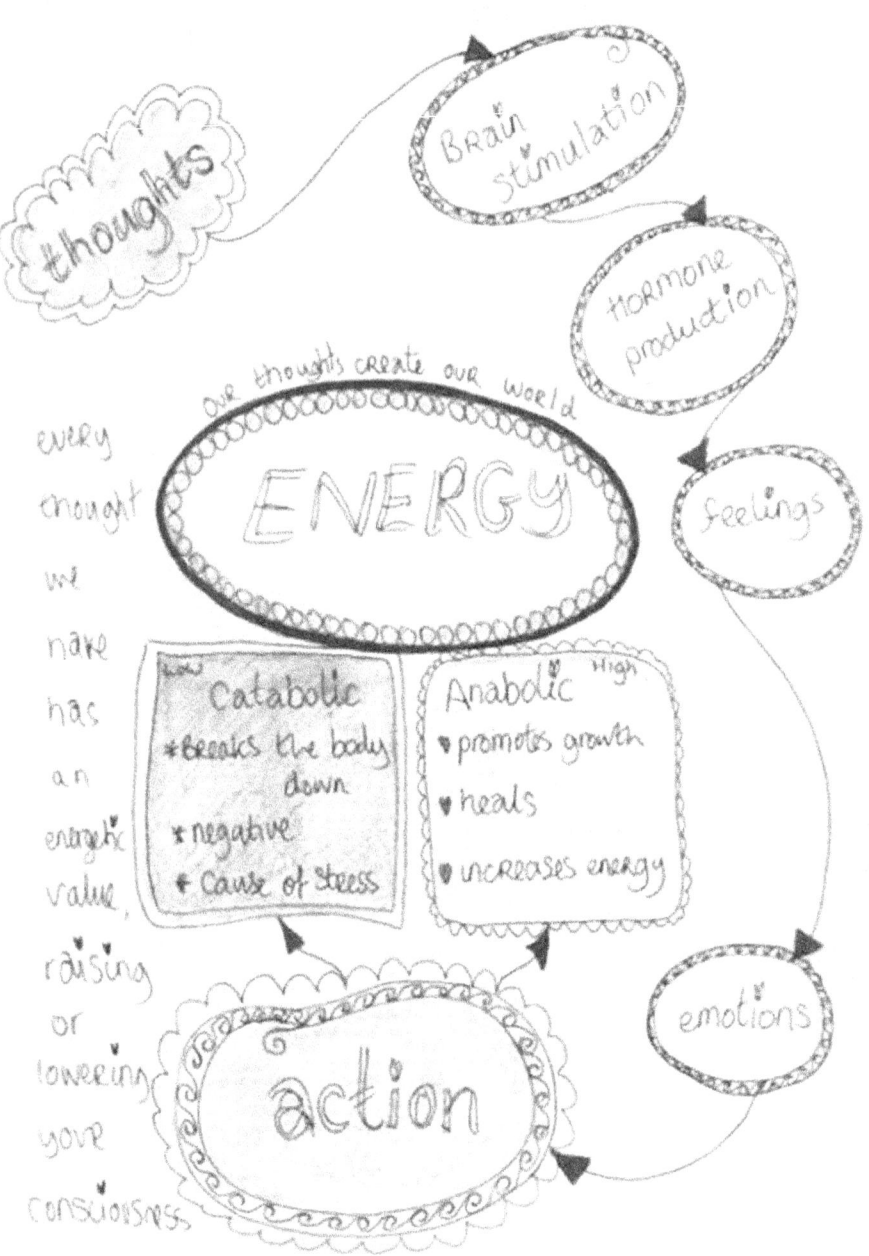

thoughts

Brain stimulation

Hormone production

feelings

Our thoughts create our world

ENERGY

every thought we have has an energetic value, raising or lowering your consciousness

Catabolic *low*
* breaks the body down
* negative
* cause of stress

Anabolic *High*
* promotes growth
* heals
* increases energy

emotions

action

Feel Good Worksheets

DATE

3 GREAT THINGS ABOUT TODAY

I FEEL SO GRATEFUL & HAPPY THAT

SOMETHING I'M LOOKING FORWARD TO

NOTES

DATE

3 GREAT THINGS ABOUT TODAY

I FEEL SO GRATEFUL & HAPPY THAT

SOMETHING I'M LOOKING FORWARD TO

NOTES

Supreme Health & Fitness!　　　　　Knowledge Of Self Series Vol 5!

PAGE 95

Creating Me!

Mirror Me

What do you see when you look in the mirror?

I see someone who is.

How Can I Improve?

Name:_____

Date:_____

Currently I can

_____

I need to improve

_____

My goal is to

_____

List ways to reach your goal:

1._____

2._____

3._____

4._____

5._____

I will achieve the goal on this date:

Supreme Health & Fitness!   Knowledge Of Self Series Vol 5!

PAGE 97

Name: _____   Date: _____

POSITIVE THOUGHTS & AFFIRMATIONS

1. There is no one better to be than myself
2. I am enough.
3. I get better every single day
4. I am an amazing person
5. All of my problems have solutions.
6. Today I am a leader.
7. I forgive myself for my mistakes.
8. My challenges help me grow
9. I am perfect just the way I am
10. My mistakes help me learn and grow.
11. Today is going to be a great day.
12. I have courage and confidence.
13. I can control my own happiness.
14. I have people who love and respect me.
15. I stand up for what I believe in
16. I believe in my goals and dreams
17. It's okay not to know everything
18. Today I choose to think positive.
19. I can get through anything.
20. I can do anything I put my mind to.
21. I give myself permission to make choices.
22. I can do better next time.
23. I have everything I need right now.
24. I am capable of so much
25. Everything will be okay.

29. I am free to make my own choices
30. I deserve to be loved.
31. I can make a difference.
32. Today I choose to be confident.
33. I am in charge of my life.
34. I have the power to make my dreams true.
35. I believe in myself and my abilities.
36. Good things are going to come to me.
37. I matter
38. My confidence grows when I step outside of my comfort zone.
39. My positive thoughts create positive feelings
40. Today I will walk through my fears.
41. I am open and ready to learn.
42. Every day is a fresh start
43. If I fail, I will get back up again.
44. I am whole.
45. I only compare myself to myself
46. I can do anything.
47. It is enough to do my best
48. I can be anything I want to be.
49. I accept who I am.
50. Today is going to be an awesome day.

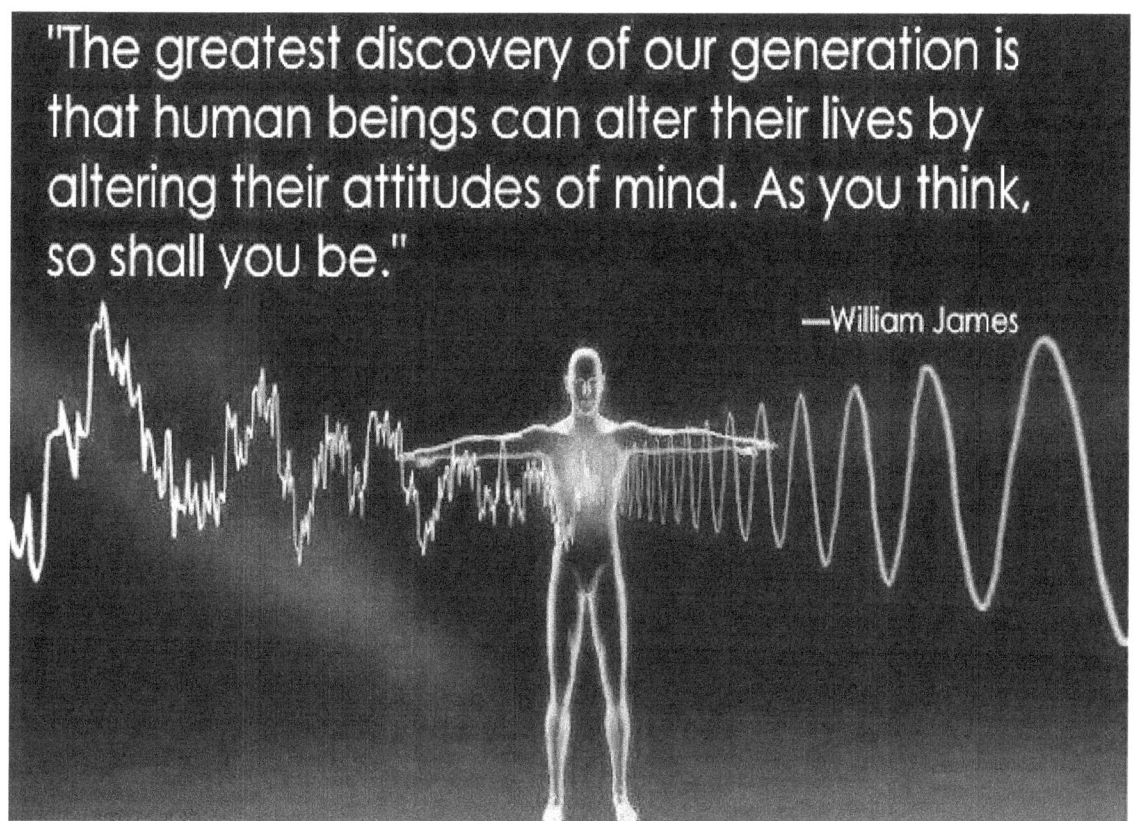

"The greatest discovery of our generation is that human beings can alter their lives by altering their attitudes of mind. As you think, so shall you be."

—William James

the **power** of words

can move you to tears, evoke absolute joy or lead you in action.

there are words of encouragement, of sympathy, of love

& admiration. the right words can give you strength, define your *faith*, give flight to things that live in your **imagination**. Words will inspire you, cut you, bring you back to life. They will comfort you in your time of need. words will

nourish your soul.

PAGE 99

Supreme Health & Fitness!   Knowledge Of Self Series Vol 5!

A strong
positive mental attitude
will create more miracles than any wonder drug.

Man, Know ThySelf ..... GOD, HEAL THYSELF!!!!

"A goal that is not written is not a goal. It only becomes real when you write it down. Look at your list daily and read it out loud. Let your list of goals become a mantra and a meditation."

Personal Development Action Plan

In order to reach your goals what behaviours will you STOP, MINIMISE, KEEP DOING, do MORE of and which will you START?

	STOP	MINIMISE	KEEP DOING	Do MORE	START
1					
2					
3					
4					
5					

Supreme Health & Fitness!　　　　　　　Knowledge Of Self Series Vol 5!

PAGE 102

90 DAY GOAL

ACTION STEPS CHECKLIST

S M A R T

MONTH 1 BENCHMARK

MONTH 2 BENCHMARK

MONTH 3 BENCHMARK

Vision Board Worksheet

Vision Board Rules

1) Goals must be true to you! Not what your family wants of you, not what society says you should be!

2) S.M.A.R.T Goals: Specific, Measurable, Attainable, Relevant, Timely.

3) State goals in a positive manner.

Instead of this...	Write this...
"I want to work out to lose weight."	"I want to work out to feel strong and sexy!"
"Stop eating junk food."	"Nourish my body with yummy home cooked meals."
"My BF and I fight less."	"My BF and I are patient and compassionate with each other."

4) Make sure your goals and the images you choose EXCITE you!

Areas of Growth

Health & Fitness	Family, Love, & Friendship	Career & Prosperity
How can I give my body the best chance?	How can I show the people closest to me that I love and appreciate them?	How can I create financial freedom doing what I love?
1	1	1
2	2	2
3	3	3
Spiritual & Knowledge	**Service & Generosity**	**Travel**
How to foster inner peace and joy?	How can I give back to the world?	How can I grow by experiencing the world?
1	1	1
2	2	2
3	3	3

And any other topic that makes you giddy!

If you find that you aren't hitting your goals, consider fewer goals that mean more to you. Break your goals into a "To-Do" list and GO FOR IT!

GOALS FOR MY MIND, BODY & SOUL

GOALS FOR MY MIND

GOALS FOR MY BODY

GOALS FOR MY SOUL

Goals for Your Mind Body & Soul

Simple Goal Setting Worksheet

The basics of setting and completing your goals

Name _____   Goal Start Date _____

MY GOAL IS: _____

_____

_____

GOAL COMPLETION DATE_____

STEPS TO REACHING MY GOAL:

1. _____

_____

2. _____

_____

3. _____

_____

4. _____

_____

TWO THINGS THAT WILL HELP ME REACH MY GOAL

1. _____

_____

_____

_____

2. _____

_____

_____

WILL KNOW I HAVE REACHED MY GOAL BECAUSE: _____

_____

_____

PAGE 106

Supreme Health & Fitness!   Knowledge Of Self Series Vol 5!

Specific. Measurable Achievable Relevant. Timely Goals

Your Goal: _____

Obstacles and Setbacks

What are the obstacles that you can foresee getting in the way of your accomplishing your goal? What are some solutions or actions that you can take to overcome these obstacles and potential setbacks?

	Obstacle or Setback	Solution and Action Item
1.		
2.		
3.		
4.		
5.		

Action Items and Tasks

List at least five action items or tasks to help you achieve your goal. Assign target dates to tasks that are not daily. (Set a target date for weekly tasks)

	Action or Task	Target Date	Completed Date
1.			
2.			
3.			
4.			
5.			
6.			
7.			

How will you reward yourself once you've accomplished your goal?

PAGE 107

Supreme Health & Fitness!   Knowledge Of Self Series Vol 5!

I got this! THIS YEAR'S GOALS

MONTH   WEEK

SPIRITUAL	LIFESTYLE	RELATIONSHIPS	FAMILY

MENTAL	PHYSICAL	FINANCIAL	BUSINESS

PAGE 108

Supreme Health & Fitness!   Knowledge Of Self Series Vol 5!

Creating Me!

WHAT AM I AIMING FOR? WHAT'S THE GOAL?

WHY IS THIS IMPORTANT TO ME? DOES IS IT ALIGN TO THE THINGS I VALUE?

WHAT AM I LETTING GET IN THE WAY OF ACHIEVING THIS GOAL?

WHAT WILL IT FEEL LIKE TO ACHIEVE THIS GOAL?

WHAT CAN I DO TODAY TO STEP CLOSER TO THIS GOAL?

Think 80% do. I need to call, what do I need to cancel, what can I delegate, what needs to be rearranged, what's the conversation that I need to have

Repeat after me....

I am Amazing and Astonishing.

I am Brilliant and Beautiful.

I am Clever, Courageous and Caring.

I am fabulous, Funny and Giving.

I am Happy, Loving and Loveable.

I am Outstanding and Sexy.

I am Terrific, Tantalising and Totally Wonderful.

I am Unique and Special and most importantly

I am ME.

ok great now say it again...

by build your confidence.

PAGE 110

Supreme Health & Fitness! Knowledge Of Self Series Vol 5!

go and love yourself

Date: _____

5 things I love about myself

1. _____
2. _____
3. _____
4. _____
5. _____

My week in feelings

10 things I'm grateful for this week

1. _____
2. _____
3. _____
4. _____
5. _____
6. _____
7. _____
8. _____
9. _____
10. _____

3 things I accomplished this week

3 things I want to accomplish next week

1. _____
2. _____
3. _____

You are awesome

A compliment to myself

PAGE 111

Supreme Health & Fitness!   Knowledge Of Self Series Vol 5!

I Feel...

I Wish...

I think...

I Need...

I Hope...

I Want...

My Strengths and Qualities

Things I am good at:

1
_____

2
_____

3
_____

Compliments I have received:

1
_____

2
_____

3
_____

What I like about my appearance:

1
_____

2
_____

3
_____

Challenges I have overcome:

1
_____

2
_____

3
_____

I've helped others by:

1
_____

2
_____

3
_____

Things that make me unique:

1
_____

2
_____

3
_____

What I value the most:

1
_____

2
_____

3
_____

Times I've made others happy:

1
_____

2
_____

3
_____

PAGE 113

Supreme Health & Fitness!   Knowledge Of Self Series Vol 5!

 # Gratitude Journal

MORNING GRATITUDE PRAYER

Before you begin your day, list 10 things you're grateful for (big or small!).

1.

2.

3.

4.

5.

6.

7.

8.

9.

10.

WHAT I'M LEARNING FROM MY CHALLENGES

List 3 challenging situations, people, or other obstacles and what good thing you're learning from this challenge.

1.

I'm learning:

2.

I'm learning:

3.

I'm learning:

PEOPLE I'M THANKFUL FOR

List 5 people who made your life a little happier today. They could be friends, family, or even strangers!

1.

2.

3.

4.

5.

THE BEST PART OF MY DAY

Choose one moment of your day that made you happy and focus on it for 5 minutes before you go to sleep.

Reflection

Date: _____

This week I did / did not make my goal. Why?

_____

_____

_____

_____

_____

Overall, I would rate my effort towards my goal:

Next Steps:

_____

_____

_____

"A goal without a plan is just a wish."

PAGE 115

Supreme Health & Fitness!   Knowledge Of Self Series Vol 5!

 # Aspiration Journal

An aspiration journal is where you write AS IF everything you want to happen in your day, week, month, year, or life has already happened. If you want a new job, don't write "I wish I had a new job." Instead, write "I love my job as Marketing Manager, and I feel so good to be sitting at my big desk in my corner office. I'm respected and liked by all my colleagues." This way you can tap into the positive feelings related to what you want and start attracting those good things to you.

ALL THE GOOD THINGS THAT HAPPENED TODAY

THE ONE THING THAT MAKES ME HAPPIEST

HOW TODAY MAKES ME FEEL

PAGE 116

Supreme Health & Fitness!   Knowledge Of Self Series Vol 5!

Challenging Negative Thoughts

Automatic negative thoughts (ANTs) only have power to affect our mood and lives if we let them. Sometimes ANTs can make things seem like a bigger deal than they really are, and those negative thoughts can affect the way you perceive and react to the situation. It is important to know how to control ANTs so they do not control you. Next time you feel a negative emotion and feel yourself about to react, consider these questions:

What happened?

_____

_____

Why is this upsetting?

_____

_____

What is the negative thought? How does it make you feel?

_____

_____

How does what happened affect the next 5 minutes? 24 hours? 7 days?

_____

_____

How does what happened affect your quality of life?

_____

_____

How much power are you giving the negative thought?

_____

_____

Does that negative thought deserve the control it has over you?

_____

_____

Next time you have this negative thought, what will you remind yourself to stay in control?

_____

_____

PAGE 117

Supreme Health & Fitness! Knowledge Of Self Series Vol 5!

daily Self love Worksheets

I **LOVE** MYSELF TODAY BECAUSE

TODAY I FORGIVE MYSELF THAT

I AM _____ BECAUSE

SOMETHING GOOD I DID FOR MYSELF TODAY

NOTES

I **LOVE** MYSELF TODAY BECAUSE

TODAY I FORGIVE MYSELF THAT

I AM _____ BECAUSE

SOMETHING GOOD I DID FOR MYSELF TODAY

NOTES

PAGE 118

Supreme Health & Fitness!   Knowledge Of Self Series Vol 5!

Self-Esteem Journal

MON.	Something I did well today...	
	Today I had fun when...	
	I felt proud when...	
TUE.	Today I accomplished...	
	I had a positive experience with...	
	Something I did for someone...	
WED.	I felt good about myself when...	
	I was proud of someone else...	
	Today was interesting because...	
THUR.	I felt proud when...	
	A positive thing I witnessed...	
	Today I accomplished...	
FRI.	Something I did well today...	
	I had a positive experience with (a person, place, or thing)...	
	I was proud of someone when...	
SAT.	Today I had fun when...	
	Something I did for someone...	
	I felt good about myself when...	
SUN.	A positive thing I witnessed...	
	Today was interesting because...	
	I felt proud when...	

PAGE 119

Supreme Health & Fitness!   Knowledge Of Self Series Vol 5!

Building Self Esteem

Month _____

	1	2	3	4	5	6	7	8	9	10	11	12	13	14	15	16	17	18	19	20	21	22	23	24	25	26	27	28	29	30	31
ACHIEVEMENTS																															
Today I helped someone else																															
Today I learned something new																															
Did something I enjoy doing																															
Received a compliment																															
Tried something outside of my comfort zone																															
Did something new																															
SELF CARE																															
Took care of personal hygiene																															
Exercised																															
Ate healthy foods																															
Today I dressed in clothes that made me feel good																															
Went outdoors																															
GOALS																															
Set a realistic goal																															
Took small step toward goal																															
Reached a goal																															
RELATIONSHIPS																															
Avoided person that makes me feel bad about myself																															
Placed my needs first																															
Protected self from an unsafe person																															
You said "No"																															

PAGE 120

Supreme Health & Fitness!   Knowledge Of Self Series Vol 5!

Positivity Pledge

I shall no longer allow negative
thoughts or feelings
to drain me of my energy.
Instead I shall focus on all the
good that is in my life.
I will think it, feel it and speak it.
By doing so I will send out
vibes of positive energy into
the world and I shall be grateful
for all the wonderful things it
will attract into my life.

PAGE 121

Supreme Health & Fitness!   Knowledge Of Self Series Vol 5!

Conclusion

14 Questions To Connect Your Mind, Body & Soul

*****

When was the last time you really checked in with yourself and took the time to really listen to your Mind, Body and Soul?

When was the last time you checked in with yourself and really took the time to understand your thoughts, feelings, dreams and desires?

We all get stuck in the trap of moving through life without really questioning what we are doing, or how we are feeling. Operating from this state however, often leaves us feeling stressed, overwhelmed and out of touch with who we truly are.

In fact, just a small check-in with yourself on a daily basis can be simple but do Wonders for your mental health, self-esteem and spiritual growth.

Since we are exploring the Self-Healing Power of Your Own Hands, with this chapter you will use your Hands to WRITE YourSelf into Your Healing, Health and Wellness!

If you are just starting out on the Path of self-discovery or already on your Journey and want to really Tune into your Mind, Body and Soul …. here are 14 great questions that can help.

These questions are designed to get you thinking about your life in a deeper and more meaningful way and at the same time be easily answered. You want to create the habit of quick-thinking about your Healing, Health and Wellness. They can also provide insights into where you are heading and where you need to focus your Time and Energy.

To work with these questions, either write down the answers in a journal, talk them through with YourSelf or use the space provided.

Creating Me!

14 Questions to Help You Connect to Your Mind, Body and Soul.

Take a deep breath. Calm your Mind and then ask yourself-

1.) What 3 words can describe how I feel right now? And Why?

1. _____
2. _____
3. _____

2.) What is going really well for me in my life right now?

_____
_____
_____
_____

3.) If I could change anything about my life what would it be?

_____
_____
_____
_____
_____

4.) What is one thing I can do to Improve my life for today?

_____
_____
_____

Creating Me!

5.) What 3 things do I LOVE about myself?

1._____
2._____
3._____

6.) What is the most Important focus of my life RIGHT NOW?

_____
_____
_____
_____

7.) What lessons have I learned this past month?

_____
_____
_____
_____

8.) What gets me Excited about Life? Is there a way I can bring more of this Energy into my daily routine?

_____
_____
_____
_____

PAGE 125

Supreme Health & Fitness!   Knowledge Of Self Series Vol 5!

9.) What is something that I have always wanted to do or try?

_____

_____

_____

10.) What do I need to Heal in my body RIGHT NOW? What are the steps I can take to make this happen?

_____

_____

_____

_____

11.) What are some things that I feel truly Grateful for RIGHT NOW?

_____

_____

_____

12.) What is one Positive Action I can do for myself RIGHT NOW?

_____

_____

_____

_____

13.) What would make me Happy RIGHT?

_____
_____
_____
_____

14.) What is the most Loving Action I can do for myself in this moment?

_____
_____
_____
_____

Answering these questions will help you to not only tune-in with yourself but it will also help you to direct the course of your Life in a way that feels Empowering and Purposeful for you RIGHT NOW and will carry-over into your future

The great thing about these questions is that they can also help you to become aware of what is working and not working in your Life so you can make the changes that you desire.

After completing these questions, you can revisit them in a few days (or sooner) and see how your answers may have shifted and changed.

Peace

Sean Ali

PAGE 127

Supreme Health & Fitness!   Knowledge Of Self Series Vol 5!

Sean Ali and 2 more

Science Of Thought & Art Of Thinking!: A Manual For Rising ABOVE Emotions! (Knowledge of Self) (Volume 1)

Format: Paperback

Sean Ali

**The God Factory - Your Brain!:
Neuroscience for the Mind of God IN
You! (Knowledge of Self) (Volume 3)**

Format: Paperback

PAGE 129

Supreme Health & Fitness!   Knowledge Of Self Series Vol 5!

Sean Ali and 2 more

Affirm * Confirm * Claim!: Writing Your Own Book of Healing, Life & Power! (Knowledge Of Self Series!) (Volume 2)

Format: Paperback

How Can I Improve?

Name:_____

Date:_____

Currently I can

I need to improve

My goal is to

List ways to reach your goal:

1._____
2._____
3._____
4._____
5._____

I will achieve the goal on this date:

How Can I Improve?

Name:_____

Date:_____

Currently I can

I need to improve

My goal is to

List ways to reach your goal:

1._____
2._____
3._____
4._____
5._____

I will achieve the goal on this date:

How I Feel

I feel: _____

Happy	Mad	Sad	Glad
Worried	Excited	Bored	Scared
Annoyed	Upset	Sick	Nervous

I feel this way because:

_____
_____
_____

This is what I did about it:

_____
_____
_____

Something else I could have done is:

_____
_____
_____

Ask for help	Take deep breaths	Walk away
Do something else	Tell an adult	Talk to a friend

How I Feel

I feel: _____

Happy	Mad	Sad	Glad
Worried	Excited	Bored	Scared
Annoyed	Upset	Sick	Nervous

I feel this way because:

_____
_____
_____

This is what I did about it:

_____
_____
_____

Something else I could have done is:

_____
_____
_____

Ask for help	Take deep breaths	Walk away
Do something else	Tell an adult	Talk to a friend

RefleCtion

Date: _____

This week I did / did not make my goal. Why?

_____

_____

_____

_____

_____

_____

Overall, I would rate my effort towards my goal:

Next Steps:

_____

_____

_____

"A goal without a plan is just a wish."

Reflection

Date: _____

This week I did / did not make my goal. Why?

_____

_____

_____

_____

_____

Overall, I would rate my effort towards my goal:

Next Steps:

_____

_____

_____

"A goal without a plan is just a wish."

Reflection

Date: _____

This week I did / did not make my goal. Why?

_____

_____

_____

_____

_____

Overall, I would rate my effort towards my goal:

Next Steps:

_____

_____

_____

"A goal without a plan is just a wish."

 # Aspiration Journal

An aspiration journal is where you write AS IF everything you want to happen in your day, week, month, year, or life has already happened. If you want a new job, don't write "I wish I had a new job." Instead, write "I love my job as Marketing Manager, and I feel so good to be sitting at my big desk in my corner office. I'm respected and liked by all my colleagues." This way you can tap into the positive feelings related to what you want and start attracting those good things to you.

ALL THE GOOD THINGS THAT HAPPENED TODAY

THE ONE THING THAT MAKES ME HAPPIEST

HOW TODAY MAKES ME FEEL

ALL THE GOOD THINGS THAT HAPPENED TODAY

THE ONE THING THAT MAKES ME HAPPIEST

HOW TODAY MAKES ME FEEL

ALL THE GOOD THINGS THAT HAPPENED TODAY

THE ONE THING THAT MAKES ME HAPPIEST

HOW TODAY MAKES ME FEEL

ALL THE GOOD THINGS THAT HAPPENED TODAY

THE ONE THING THAT MAKES ME HAPPIEST

HOW TODAY MAKES ME FEEL

daily Self love Worksheets

I LOVE MYSELF TODAY BECAUSE ...

TODAY I FORGIVE MYSELF THAT ...

I AM _____ BECAUSE ...

SOMETHING GOOD I DID FOR MYSELF TODAY

NOTES

I LOVE MYSELF TODAY BECAUSE ...

TODAY I FORGIVE MYSELF THAT ...

I AM _____ BECAUSE ...

SOMETHING GOOD I DID FOR MYSELF TODAY

NOTES

PAGE 142

Supreme Health & Fitness!   Knowledge Of Self Series Vol 5!

daily Self love Worksheets

I LOVE MYSELF TODAY BECAUSE

TODAY I FORGIVE MYSELF THAT

I AM   BECAUSE

SOMETHING GOOD I DID FOR MYSELF TODAY

NOTES

I LOVE MYSELF TODAY BECAUSE

TODAY I FORGIVE MYSELF THAT

I AM   BECAUSE

SOMETHING GOOD I DID FOR MYSELF TODAY

NOTES

PAGE | 43

Supreme Health & Fitness!   Knowledge Of Self Series Vol 5!

daily Self love Worksheets

I LOVE MYSELF TODAY BECAUSE

TODAY I FORGIVE MYSELF THAT

I AM _____ BECAUSE

SOMETHING GOOD I DID FOR MYSELF TODAY

NOTES

I LOVE MYSELF TODAY BECAUSE

TODAY I FORGIVE MYSELF THAT

I AM _____ BECAUSE

SOMETHING GOOD I DID FOR MYSELF TODAY

NOTES

PAGE 144

Supreme Health & Fitness!   Knowledge Of Self Series Vol 5!

Self-Esteem Journal

MON.	Something I did well today...	
	Today I had fun when...	
	I felt proud when...	
TUE.	Today I accomplished...	
	I had a positive experience with...	
	Something I did for someone...	
WED.	I felt good about myself when...	
	I was proud of someone else...	
	Today was interesting because...	
THUR.	I felt proud when...	
	A positive thing I witnessed...	
	Today I accomplished...	
FRI.	Something I did well today...	
	I had a positive experience with (a person, place, or thing)...	
	I was proud of someone when...	
SAT.	Today I had fun when...	
	Something I did for someone...	
	I felt good about myself when...	
SUN.	A positive thing I witnessed...	
	Today was interesting because...	
	I felt proud when...	

Self-Esteem Journal

MON.	Something I did well today...	
	Today I had fun when...	
	I felt proud when...	
TUE.	Today I accomplished...	
	I had a positive experience with...	
	Something I did for someone...	
WED.	I felt good about myself when...	
	I was proud of someone else...	
	Today was interesting because...	
THUR.	I felt proud when...	
	A positive thing I witnessed...	
	Today I accomplished...	
FRI.	Something I did well today...	
	I had a positive experience with (a person, place, or thing)...	
	I was proud of someone when...	
SAT.	Today I had fun when...	
	Something I did for someone...	
	I felt good about myself when...	
SUN.	A positive thing I witnessed...	
	Today was interesting because...	
	i felt proud when...	

PAGE 146

Supreme Health & Fitness!   Knowledge Of Self Series Vol 5!

Self-Esteem Journal

MON.	Something I did well today...	
	Today I had fun when...	
	I felt proud when...	
TUE.	Today I accomplished...	
	I had a positive experience with...	
	Something I did for someone...	
WED.	I felt good about myself when...	
	I was proud of someone else...	
	Today was interesting because...	
THUR.	I felt proud when...	
	A positive thing I witnessed...	
	Today I accomplished...	
FRI.	Something I did well today...	
	I had a positive experience with (a person, place, or thing)...	
	I was proud of someone when...	
SAT.	Today I had fun when...	
	Something I did for someone...	
	I felt good about myself when...	
SUN.	A positive thing I witnessed...	
	Today was interesting because...	
	I felt proud when...	

PAGE 147

Supreme Health & Fitness!   Knowledge Of Self Series Vol 5!

 # Gratitude Journal

MORNING GRATITUDE PRAYER

Before you begin your day, list 10 things you're grateful for (big or small!).

1.

2.

3.

4.

5.

6.

7.

8.

9.

10.

WHAT I'M LEARNING FROM MY CHALLENGES

List 3 challenging situations, people, or other obstacles and what good thing you're learning from this challenge.

1.

I'm learning:

2.

I'm learning:

3.

I'm learning:

PEOPLE I'M THANKFUL FOR

List 5 people who made your life a little happier today. They could be friends, family, or even strangers!

1.

2.

3.

4.

5.

THE BEST PART OF MY DAY

Choose one moment of your day that made you happy and focus on it for 5 minutes before you go to sleep.

MORNING GRATITUDE PRAYER

Before you begin your day, list 10 things you're grateful for (big or small!).

1.

2.

3.

4.

5.

6.

7.

8.

9.

10.

WHAT I'M LEARNING FROM MY CHALLENGES

List 3 challenging situations, people, or other obstacles and what good thing you're learning from this challenge.

1.

I'm learning:

2.

I'm learning:

3.

I'm learning:

PEOPLE I'M THANKFUL FOR

List 5 people who made your life a little happier today. They could be friends, family, or even strangers!

1.

2.

3.

4.

5.

THE BEST PART OF MY DAY

Choose one moment of your day that made you happy and focus on it for 5 minutes before you go to sleep.

PAGE 149

Supreme Health & Fitness!   Knowledge Of Self Series Vol 5!

MORNING GRATITUDE PRAYER

Before you begin your day, list 10 things you're grateful for (big or small!).

1.

2.

3.

4.

5.

6.

7.

8.

9.

10.

WHAT I'M LEARNING FROM MY CHALLENGES

List 3 challenging situations, people, or other obstacles and what good thing you're learning from this challenge.

1.

I'm learning:

2.

I'm learning:

3.

I'm learning:

PEOPLE I'M THANKFUL FOR

List 5 people who made your life a little happier today. They could be friends, family, or even strangers!

1.

2.

3.

4.

5.

THE BEST PART OF MY DAY

Choose one moment of your day that made you happy and focus on it for 5 minutes before you go to sleep.

PAGE 150

Supreme Health & Fitness!   Knowledge Of Self Series Vol 5!

MORNING GRATITUDE PRAYER

Before you begin your day, list 10 things you're grateful for (big or small!).

1.

2.

3.

4.

5.

6.

7.

8.

9.

10.

WHAT I'M LEARNING FROM MY CHALLENGES

List 3 challenging situations, people, or other obstacles and what good thing you're learning from this challenge.

1.

I'm learning:

2.

I'm learning:

3.

I'm learning:

PEOPLE I'M THANKFUL FOR

List 5 people who made your life a little happier today. They could be friends, family, or even strangers!

1.

2.

3.

4.

5.

THE BEST PART OF MY DAY

Choose one moment of your day that made you happy and focus on it for 5 minutes before you go to sleep.

Challenging Negative Thoughts

Automatic negative thoughts (ANTs) only have power to affect our mood and lives if we let them. Sometimes ANTs can make things seem like a bigger deal than they really are, and those negative thoughts can affect the way you perceive and react to the situation. It is important to know how to control ANTs so they do not control you. Next time you feel a negative emotion and feel yourself about to react, consider these questions:

What happened?

_____

_____

Why is this upsetting?

_____

_____

What is the negative thought? How does it make you feel?

_____

_____

How does what happened affect the next 5 minutes? 24 hours? 7 days?

_____

_____

How does what happened affect your quality of life?

_____

_____

How much power are you giving the negative thought?

_____

_____

Does that negative thought deserve the control it has over you?

_____

_____

Next time you have this negative thought, what will you remind yourself to stay in control?

_____

_____

PAGE 152

Supreme Health & Fitness!   Knowledge Of Self Series Vol 5!

Challenging Negative Thoughts

Automatic negative thoughts (ANTs) only have power to affect our mood and lives if we let them. Sometimes ANTs can make things seem like a bigger deal than they really are, and those negative thoughts can affect the way you perceive and react to the situation. It is important to know how to control ANTs so they do not control you. Next time you feel a negative emotion and feel yourself about to react, consider these questions:

What happened?

_____

_____

Why is this upsetting?

_____

_____

What is the negative thought? How does it make you feel?

_____

_____

How does what happened affect the next 5 minutes? 24 hours? 7 days?

_____

_____

How does what happened affect your quality of life?

_____

_____

How much power are you giving the negative thought?

_____

_____

Does that negative thought deserve the control it has over you?

_____

_____

Next time you have this negative thought, what will you remind yourself to stay in control?

_____

_____

Challenging Negative Thoughts

Automatic negative thoughts (ANTs) only have power to affect our mood and lives if we let them. Sometimes ANTs can make things seem like a bigger deal than they really are, and those negative thoughts can affect the way you perceive and react to the situation. It is important to know how to control ANTs so they do not control you. Next time you feel a negative emotion and feel yourself about to react, consider these questions:

What happened?

_____

_____

Why is this upsetting?

_____

_____

What is the negative thought? How does it make you feel?

_____

_____

How does what happened affect the next 5 minutes? 24 hours? 7 days?

_____

_____

How does what happened affect your quality of life?

_____

_____

How much power are you giving the negative thought?

_____

_____

Does that negative thought deserve the control it has over you?

_____

_____

Next time you have this negative thought, what will you remind yourself to stay in control?

_____

_____

Personal Development Action Plan

In order to reach your goals what behaviours will you STOP, MINIMISE, KEEP DOING, do MORE of and which will you START?

	STOP	MINIMISE	KEEP DOING	Do MORE	START
1					
2					
3					
4					
5					

Personal Development Action Plan

In order to reach your goals what behaviours will you STOP, MINIMISE, KEEP DOING, do MORE of and which will you START?

	STOP	MINIMISE	KEEP DOING	Do MORE	START
1					
2					
3					
4					
5					

PAGE 156

Supreme Health & Fitness!   Knowledge Of Self Series Vol 5!

Personal Development Action Plan

In order to reach your goals what behaviours will you STOP, MINIMISE, KEEP DOING, do MORE of and which will you START?

	STOP	MINIMISE	KEEP DOING	Do MORE	START
1					
2					
3					
4					
5					

PAGE 157

Supreme Health & Fitness!   Knowledge Of Self Series Vol 5!

Building Self Esteem

Month _____

	1	2	3	4	5	6	7	8	9	10	11	12	13	14	15	16	17	18	19	20	21	22	23	24	25	26	27	28	29	30	31
ACHIEVEMENTS																															
Today I helped someone else																															
Today I learned something new																															
Did something I enjoy doing																															
Received a compliment																															
Tried something outside of my comfort zone																															
Did something new																															
SELF CARE																															
Took care of personal hygiene																															
Exercised																															
Ate healthy foods																															
Today I dressed in clothes that made me feel good																															
Went outdoors																															
GOALS																															
Set a realistic goal																															
Took small step toward goal																															
Reached a goal																															
RELATIONSHIPS																															
Avoided person that makes me feel bad about myself																															
Placed my needs first																															
Protected self from an unsafe person																															
You said "No"																															

PAGE 158

Supreme Health & Fitness!   Knowledge Of Self Series Vol 5!

Building Self Esteem

Month _____

	1	2	3	4	5	6	7	8	9	10	11	12	13	14	15	16	17	18	19	20	21	22	23	24	25	26	27	28	29	30	31
ACHIEVEMENTS																															
Today I helped someone else																															
Today I learned something new																															
Did something I enjoy doing																															
Received a compliment																															
Tried something outside of my comfort zone																															
Did something new																															
SELF CARE																															
Took care of personal hygiene																															
Exercised																															
Ate healthy foods																															
Today I dressed in clothes that made me feel good																															
Went outdoors																															
GOALS																															
Set a realistic goal																															
Took small step toward goal																															
Reached a goal																															
RELATIONSHIPS																															
Avoided person that makes me feel bad about myself																															
Placed my needs first																															
Protected self from an unsafe person																															
You said 'No'																															

PAGE 159

Supreme Health & Fitness!   Knowledge Of Self Series Vol 5!

Building Self Esteem

Month _____

	1	2	3	4	5	6	7	8	9	10	11	12	13	14	15	16	17	18	19	20	21	22	23	24	25	26	27	28	29	30	31
ACHIEVEMENTS																															
Today I helped someone else																															
Today I learned something new																															
Did something I enjoy doing																															
Received a compliment																															
Tried something outside of my comfort zone																															
Did something new																															
SELF CARE																															
Took care of personal hygiene																															
Exercised																															
Ate healthy foods																															
Today I dressed in clothes that made me feel good																															
Went outdoors																															
GOALS																															
Set a realistic goal																															
Took small step toward goal																															
Reached a goal																															
RELATIONSHIPS																															
Avoided person that makes me feel bad about myself																															
Placed my needs first																															
Protected self from an unsafe person																															
You said "No"																															

PAGE 160

Supreme Health & Fitness!　　　　Knowledge Of Self Series Vol 5!

Building Self Esteem

Month _____

	1	2	3	4	5	6	7	8	9	10	11	12	13	14	15	16	17	18	19	20	21	22	23	24	25	26	27	28	29	30	31
ACHIEVEMENTS																															
Today I helped someone else																															
Today I learned something new																															
Did something I enjoy doing																															
Received a compliment																															
Tried something outside of my comfort zone																															
Did something new																															
SELF CARE																															
Took care of personal hygiene																															
Exercised																															
Ate healthy foods																															
Today I dressed in clothes that made me feel good																															
Went outdoors																															
GOALS																															
Set a realistic goal																															
Took small step toward goal																															
Reached a goal																															
RELATIONSHIPS																															
Avoided person that makes me feel bad about myself																															
Placed my needs first																															
Protected self from an unsafe person																															
You said "No"																															

PAGE 161

Supreme Health & Fitness!   Knowledge Of Self Series Vol 5!

I FeeL...

I WiSH...

I tHiNK...

I Need...

I HoPe...

I WaNt...

PAGE 162

Supreme Health & Fitness!   Knowledge Of Self Series Vol 5!

I FeeL...

I WiSH...

I tHiNK...

I Need...

I Hope...

I WaNt...

PAGE 163

Supreme Health & Fitness!   Knowledge Of Self Series Vol 5!

go and love yourself

Date: _____

5 things I love about myself

1. _____
2. _____
3. _____
4. _____
5. _____

My week in feelings

10 things I'm grateful for this week

1. _____
2. _____
3. _____
4. _____
5. _____
6. _____
7. _____
8. _____
9. _____
10. _____

3 things I accomplished this week

3 things I want to accomplish next week

1. _____
2. _____
3. _____

You are awesome

A compliment to myself

PAGE 164

Supreme Health & Fitness!   Knowledge Of Self Series Vol 5!

go and love yourself

Date: _____

5 things I love about myself

1. _____
2. _____
3. _____
4. _____
5. _____

My week in feelings

10 things I'm grateful for this week

1. _____
2. _____
3. _____
4. _____
5. _____
6. _____
7. _____
8. _____
9. _____
10. _____

3 things I accomplished this week

3 things I want to accomplish next week

1. _____
2. _____
3. _____

You are awesome

A compliment to myself

go and love yourself

Date: _____

5 things I love about myself

1. _____
2. _____
3. _____
4. _____
5. _____

My week in feelings

10 things I'm grateful for this week

1. _____
2. _____
3. _____
4. _____
5. _____
6. _____
7. _____
8. _____
9. _____
10. _____

3 things I accomplished this week

3 things I want to accomplish next week

1. _____
2. _____
3. _____

You are awesome

A compliment to myself

PAGE 166

Supreme Health & Fitness!   Knowledge Of Self Series Vol 5!

go and love yourself

Date: _____

5 things I love about myself

1. _____
2. _____
3. _____
4. _____
5. _____

My week in feelings

10 things I'm grateful for this week

1. _____
2. _____
3. _____
4. _____
5. _____
6. _____
7. _____
8. _____
9. _____
10. _____

3 things I accomplished this week

3 things I want to accomplish next week

1. _____
2. _____
3. _____

you are awesome

A compliment to myself

Conclusion

Love Letter to Your Future Self!

*****

DEAR FUTURE SELF...

Write a letter to your future self applying insight gained from the personality assessments you have taken over the last week. What did you learn about yourself? What aspects of your personality do you hope are stable? What aspects do you hope to change and how?

Your letter should address a humanistic perspective, trait theory, and social-cognitive.

This is your chance to write your history in Advance and Walk Right Into It!

Its YOUR Life …. It is designed to Be exactly what you want it to Be!

It's All Up To YOU!!!

PAGE 169

Supreme Health & Fitness!   Knowledge Of Self Series Vol 5!

PAGE 173

Supreme Health & Fitness!   Knowledge Of Self Series Vol 5!

Creating Me!

Creating Me!